Models
of Black
Theology

Models
of Black
Theology

Issues in
Class, Culture,
and Gender

Julian Kunnie
//

TRINITY PRESS INTERNATIONAL
Valley Forge, Pennsylvania

Acknowledgment is gratefully given for permission to reprint from the following:

A. C. Jordan, *Tales from Southern Africa*, "Nomabhadi and the Mbulu Makhasana," pages 155–79, copyright © 1973 The Regents of the University of California.

"Afro-American Fragment," from *Selected Poems* by Langston Hughes, copyright © 1959 by Langston Hughes, reprinted by permission of Alfred A. Knopf, Inc.

Trinity Press International,
P.O. Box 851, Valley Forge, PA 19482-0851

Cover design: Ife Designs

Library of Congress Cataloging-in-Publication Data

Kunnie, Julian.
   Models of black theology : issues in class, culture, and
gender / by Julian Kunnie. — 1st ed.
      p. cm.
   Includes bibliographical references and index.
   ISBN 1-56338-088-9 :
   1. Black theology. 2. Liberation theology. 3. Sociology,
Christian — United States. 4. Sociology, Christian — South Africa.
5. Cone, James H. 6. Tutu, Desmond. I. Title.
BT82.7.K86 1994
230'.08996 — dc20
                                                      94-9169
                                                      CIP

Printed in the United States of America

94   95   96   97   98   99   10   9   8   7   6   5   4   3   2   1

For My Loving Father,
Matthew Kunnie,
December 21, 1921–July 6, 1989
who taught me what struggle in life really means
and how love can conquer all evil.

Contents

Preface

Ground for a revolution is always fertile in the presence of ab-
solute destitution. At some stage one can foresee a situation
where black people will feel that they have nothing to live for
and will shout unto their God "Thy will be done." Indeed His
will shall be done but it shall not appeal equally to all mortals
for indeed we have different versions of His will. If the white
God has been doing the talking all along, at some stage the
black God will have to raise His voice and make Himself heard
over and above the noises from his counterpart. What happens at that stage depends largely on what happens in the
intervening period. "Black consciousness" therefore seeks to
give positivity in the outlook of the black people to their prob-
lems. It works on the knowledge that "white hatred" is negative,
though understandable, and leads to precipitate and shot-gun
methods which may be disastrous for black and white alike.
It seeks to channel the pent-up forces of the angry black
masses to meaningful and directional opposition basing its entire struggle on realities of the situation. It wants to ensure a
singularity of purpose in the minds of the black people and
to make possible total involvement of the masses in a struggle
essentially theirs.

—*Steve Biko, I Write What I Like*

It is 1994, just six years from the turn of the millennium. Black
people and other indigenous peoples of color who have been colonized are still not free to define who they are and to determine their
own destiny. If the absurdity of contemporary black experience of
subjugation is one indicator of the successes of modern civilization,
many black people may yet opt to dissociate themselves from this
civilization and become "uncivilized"!

This book represents an attempt to make sense of the crucible of
black struggle in the face of the anomaly of black suffering in the
nineties. It may be a disturbing book because it makes some radi-

cal pronouncements on the pathologies of racism, colonization, and capitalist exploitation, criticisms that are not in vogue with many mainstream critics of either the "right" or the "left." It endeavors to communicate what is perceived to be the truth of black experience. It re-embraces the philosophy of black consciousness, even though many black and white people in the United States and South Africa have dismissed this philosophy as anachronistic for current socio-political struggles of liberation. It argues for the right of all colonized indigenous peoples to evolve their own methodologies of liberation in the building of participatory democratic socialistic societies, even though socialism has been eschewed and become the laughing-stock of much of the capitalist world today. This book does not simply critique capitalism and propose socialism; rather, it suggests dipping into the wellspring of indigenous black working class culture and examines issues of cosmology, sacredness of land, respect for community, and the alienation wrought by materialism and consumerism from the standpoint of indigenous peoples, while realizing that socialism does not necessarily embrace all of these concerns.

A recurring theme in this book is the eruption of indigenous culture and experience in the doing of Christian theology and the challenge that such culture presents to the Christian tradition. Can Christianity embrace such a radical faith expression and accept the power of indigenous tradition in informing Christian teaching and life? What are the implications for Christians and other religious people in the United States and around the world? Can we still build a nonracist, just, and free world when there are such variances of experience between the have's and have-not's? This book is part of black theology's endeavor to respond positively to these questions and to help build bridges across racial and class lines, difficult as this task is.

In an intellectual sense, then, *Models of Black Theology* appears to be out-of-step with prevailing reality, at least as defined by the dominant culture. This is precisely the reason that it warrants reading. It reflects a viewpoint that many black people in the world share, representing the voices, feelings, and aspirations of many oppressed indigenous peoples who have never had the opportunity to articulate their views in book form, for whatever reason.

The message in this book emanates from a critical black perspective based on my experiences in the United States and South Africa. I have been involved in black struggles for liberation in these contexts for several years, and have undertaken extensive academic research in the areas of race, politics, and theology. This book is the product of intense reflection, prayer, and thought over the years. It is intended to deepen the discussion on black religious and social experience, notwithstanding its sometimes provocative style. While the book is primarily didactic in character and geared toward offering constructive insights for advancing the black liberation project, it is also an invitation to dialogue with all persons earnestly committed to fundamental social change.

Acknowledgments

The African adage *Umuntu Ungumuntu Ngabantu Ngabanye* in the Zulu language of South Africa and *Motho ke Motho ka Batho* in the Sotho tongue translates as "a person is, only because of, and with others." This book was certainly not made possible by my efforts alone.

I want to express my appreciation to the Great Spirit for powerfully inspiring my determination in the writing of this book, to the indigenous Indian people of the United States for hosting me in this country, and to the black people of America and of South Africa whose indomitable courage in the struggle for liberation has refreshed me in my miles of research and study.

Special thanks go to my family, especially my wife, Kim, for her rigorous proofreading and editing of the text amid all her pastoral responsibilities, even while being a wonderful mother to our beautiful infant son, Mandla. I am indebted to my mother, Magdaline, sister Lorna, and brothers, Lionel and Michael, for their encouragement of my work from afar in South Africa.

I also want to express my gratitude to my colleagues in the Department of Theology at Valparaiso University, particularly Walt Rast, who suggested that I submit my manuscript to Trinity Press International for publication. I am grateful to the Dean of the College of Arts and Sciences at Valparaiso University, Philip Gilbertson, who has been extremely supportive of my research and scholarly pursuits. My mentor at the Pacific School of Religion in Berkeley, California, who chaired the committee of my doctoral dissertation, Choan-Seng Song, warrants mention for his nurture of my personal theological development that led to the publishing of this book.

Finally, I would like to acknowledge my appreciation to Harold Rast, publisher of Trinity Press International, who stayed with me throughout my editing of the text. His suggestions and comments have not only helped me produce a more refined manuscript, but also made me a more skillful writer in the process.

Introduction

Only two societies in recent history, the United States and South Africa, have practiced *de jure* segregation based on race. The United States, of course, is infamous for its Jim Crow racial separation legislation prior to the sixties; South Africa is notorious for its hideous system of racial oppression called apartheid. Through the past three centuries, black people in the United States and South Africa have been distinctively connected by the evolution of human history on the American and African continents, respectively.

The emergence of black theology in recent years has been helpful in the illumination of the incompatibility of racism and its effects with the notion of divinity, and in particular, with the mandate of the Christian gospel. Further, black theology has been instrumental in empowering black people to assert their right to religious self-determination and to demand justice and liberation from societal, political, and economic structures of oppression and domination. It has also provided avenues of faith-practice for black religious communities seeking greater insight into what it means to be black in the world.

Yet begging questions remain. Why does racism persist in this world, and why are black people unable to wrest themselves from racist oppression even after the repeal of racist legislation in places like the United States and, more recently, in South Africa? In essence, why do black people continue to suffer the indignity of racism and the humiliation of being second-class citizens in a supposedly modern and civilized world? Even more perplexing, why do religious people who are believers in the power of God's Spirit and deliverance by the Holy Spirit continue to languish in the maelstrom of oppression and degradation? Further, how does one affirm a life-giving God in a world in which the humanity of black people is trampled on and the lives of black people are threatened by racism?

These pointed questions compel black theologians to probe the depths of racist oppression in an effort to understand its fundamental causes and to propose appropriate theological responses by communities of faith. Such engagement necessitates that black theologians develop an indigenous methodology of social and historical analysis that will enable them to fathom the tenacity of racism. By indigenous methodology I mean a primary dependence on native black resources and ingredients that are drawn from and particularly relevant to black history and experience, with a secondary reliance upon nonblack sources.

One of the principal operating assumptions in this book is that religion is a response to specific historical and social events and processes. Religion is influenced by history and culture, just as it affects both history and culture. Theology, as critical reflection on religious experience, thus draws upon both history and culture. Black theology, as one expression of theology, must also recognize the social and historical character of black religious faith, so as to understand the complexity of black personal and communal life.

A social analysis methodology in black theology implies the utilization of the disciplines of the social sciences, such as history, sociology, economics, political science, and psychology, in the explanation of the contents of black religious faith and in relating black spirituality to the material struggle for liberation. It entails delving into the history of black societies to understand the historical, political, social, economic, and cultural structures that have led to the crisis of black suffering today and possibly to discover indigenous historical sources that could be used in the contemporary resistance to this oppression. It also involves situating the microcosm of black experience within the wider context of national society and macrocosm of global development, underscoring that what the world does affects black people and conversely. Consequently, it attempts to furnish some substantive intellectual resources for clarifying and deepening the understanding of black spirituality, so that black religious faith can be strengthened for the purpose of transforming the material reality of black oppression. Social analysis in black theology, therefore, subscribes to the notion that procuring knowledge is a precondition for the acquisition of power to be able to define black reality. The black struggle for liberation also implies struggle at the discursive level: to be able to describe the truth about this world from the vantage point of oppressed black experience.

In today's age of intellectual sophistication and technological complexity, it is inadequate to rally around the banner of blackness without qualifying the manner of blackness. Black identity must become transformed into a dynamic course of black liberation of oppressed black peoples and, ineluctably, of their oppressors, for the purpose of building genuinely nonracist, just, and participatory societies. Being black and being theological is not enough. The recurring question is: how can black theology develop an indigenous social analysis methodology that can be used as an effective instrument for black liberation?

In this book I examine this question of social analysis and its use in black theology, especially with regard to the issues of class, culture, and gender as categories of oppression. An equally relevant question is that of the theological and ecclesiastical dimensions of racism, its history, and the manner that the ideology of racism and religion of western European Christendom have converged to accept and even legitimate the practice of exploitation of black people in the United States and South Africa.

It was the context of black survival against oppression for over three hundred years that spawned the emergence of black theologies of liberation. The response of resistance to racist oppression by black peoples is very much a part of the practice of black theology. I therefore begin with the chronology of the black struggle against racism in the United States and South Africa. With regard to the South African situation, I take issue with the current developments toward change and sound a caveat against overly optimistic perceptions. From the vantage point of the apartheid system, tremendous changes have occurred. From the perspective of oppressed black people, no substantive change has transpired because the apartheid regime has not surrendered power and is not at the precipice of doing so.

Following this examination of the social history of black people in the United States and South Africa, I describe elements of social analysis in the work of two black theologians, James Cone and Desmond Tutu, with regard to liberation from oppression. James Cone gave prominence to the black theology enterprise in the 1960s with his groundbreaking work, *Black Theology and Black Power*. There he argued that the notion of black power is consistent with a black theology of liberation. Since that work, Cone has written on a variety of topics, including black theology's relation to the black church, feminist theology, Marxism, liberation theologies in Africa, Asia, and Latin America, and the relevance of Martin Luther King, Jr., and Malcolm X in black liberation struggles. Cone is important especially because he proposes the use of social analysis in black theology, a subject that he explained in *For My People* (1984). His life as an academic theologian, his membership in the African Methodist Episcopal Church and the United Methodist Church, his passionate love for the black church, and his involvement in the international sphere through organizations such as the Ecumenical Association of Third World Theologians (EATWOT) make him an important theologian for consideration in the advancing of the current black liberation struggle.

Desmond Tutu has for many years been in the forefront of the church battle against apartheid rule in South Africa. His commitment to the cause of liberation in South Africa through nonviolent means won him the Nobel Peace Prize in 1984. He is currently the archbishop of Cape Town and the leader of the Anglican church in southern Africa. As an African, Tutu brings some distinctive cultural features to the black theology movement. In addition, he is a practical theologian who has been involved in protests against the apartheid system in South Africa and is one of apartheid's most vocal critics. Tutu's prophetic role as a clergyperson and his consciousness of socio-economic factors in theological exploration make his writings worth considering as a model of black theology.

Finally, I propose an indigenous black social analysis methodology that can be instructive for black religious and social empowerment, especially for the faith practice of the Christian church and other religious communities in their support of human liberation and transformation. My critique of the black church is intended to be constructive, rooted in a profound passion for this dynamic religious community and based on over two decades of experience in black churches. It is by no measure geared toward "putting down" the black church or conjuring negative impressions of black churches, but is for the purpose of assisting the black church in becoming most effective in its prophetic proclamation of the Christian gospel. The methodology proposed in this book utilizes the indigenous black folk tale and proceeds to demonstrate how such analysis can be concretely done. It suggests some specific implications for black churches in the United States and South Africa. The issues of class, culture, and gender have never been discussed in such detail in a black theological text before, with nexuses to the original inhabitants of this land, the indigenous people, and the environmental movement.

Models of Black Theology is geared toward bridging the chasm between black experiences in the United States and South Africa. Black people in the United States must reach out to embrace Africa and recover their long-lost African heritage in an intentional and profound way, not in some vague and superficial manner. This dimension is crucial in addressing the crisis of black identity and experience in America. South Africa may have some answers in this regard, hence the bonding of both contexts.

Chapter 1

The Struggle Against Racism

So long
So far away
Is Africa.
Not even memories alive
Save those that history books create,
Save those that songs
Beat back into the blood —
Beat out of blood with words sad-sung
In strange unNegro tongue —
So long,
So far away
Is Africa.

—*Langston Hughes, Afro-American Fragment*[1]

Black theology has emerged in response to European and Euro-American theologies that have either largely ignored black experience or excluded it from the domain of theology. Black theology therefore tapped into the wellspring of the history of resistance to racism as one source for its thesis of liberation. The raison d'être of black theology, in fact, is the tenacity of racism and its clever subversion of the reality that black humanity is indeed created in God's image. The problem of persistent racism requires that the historical experiences of black oppression be probed and its root causes understood so that prescriptions for its abolition can be suggested. The ultimate goal of black theology, therefore, is the construction of authentically nonracist societies.

---

1. Cited in *Black Voices: An Anthology of Afro-American Literature,* ed. Abraham Chapman (New York and Scarborough, Ontario: New American Library, 1968), 425.

The United States:
A History of Racist Oppression

Lerone Bennett explains in his informative work *Before the May-flower* that the historical genesis of black people in the United States did not begin at Plymouth Rock in 1620, as it did for white people. Rather, it can be traced to the violent disruptions that emerged with the trans-Atlantic slave trade and the first passage of African slaves in the early 1600s. This forced migration in the aftermath of the Portuguese slave trade brought half a million Africans to Spanish America by 1650.[2] The presence of black people in the early 1500s in Latin America and subsequently in North America in the 1600s occurred in the wake of the virtual decimation of the native American population in North America, parts of South America, and the Caribbean islands.

By the middle of the fifteenth century, amid the thriving trade relations between Europe and West Africa, a novel and gruesome institution surfaced in the trade of African women and men in the form of chattel slavery by Europeans. Europeans sought the purchase of Africans from their African trading partners, mostly along the coastal areas of West Africa — Benin, Oyo, Dahomey, Akwamu, and Ashanti. European merchants realized that the purchase and sale of African people would accrue enormous profits, since slaves could be sold at fifty to one hundred percent more than their purchase price.[3]

The first Africans who came to America's shores via the Middle Passage, the journey between the West African coast and the United States, did not come as immigrants, as all other peoples who settled in the United States save the native Americans. They came instead, as forced chattel slaves. The Middle Passage was among the most inhumane, brutal and unbearable journeys of recent history.[4] The fatality rate among Africans during these trans-Atlantic crossings averaged thirteen percent and was wrought mainly through suicide by Africans who jumped overboard rather than be subjected to the humiliation of slavery. Many lives were also lost through shipwrecks on turbulent seas.

August 1619 marked the first purchase of African slaves in North America by the colonists in Jamestown, Virginia. The first group of Africans who landed at Jamestown were indentured servants. Africans became a commodity for exploitative labor in Maryland in

---

2. Cedric Robinson, *Black Marxism* (London: Zed Press, 1983), 155.
3. Ibid., 17.
4. Ibid., 18.

the 1630s, in Carolina in 1669, and in New England and Massachusetts around the same period. Tobacco plantations in the New England area, for instance, called for involuntary labor because of the shortage of voluntary labor. Interestingly, Virginia had minimal contact with the Spanish, Portuguese, and Dutch colonies and the other English colonies engaging in African slavery, yet proceeded to adopt the exploitative practice of slavery nonetheless. Legalization of slavery followed its social practice, and by 1660 slavery had become statutory law in the colonies.[5] Europeans were also forced to work as servants, but their period of servitude was limited. Africans, on the other hand, were institutionalized servants for life, and their freedom was possible only through the favorable death wills of slaveholders.

Why were African people singled out for chattel slavery? Why were European traders and merchants not content with Irish, Dutch, or Spanish servants, all of whom were transferred to American shores simultaneously with African women and men? In the incipient stages of slavery, the British distinguished themselves as Christians and proud Englishmen, in contrast to Africans, who were considered uncivilized heathens. To be Christian was to be civilized and refined; to be African was to be barbaric. Thus Christianity became equated with European ethnicity. Through the seventeenth and eighteenth centuries, however, color differences and physiological characteristics rather than religious heritage became decisive in the legitimation of slavery, and the factor of blackness functioned as a convenient category for dehumanizing African peoples by evoking historically negative associations with blackness, such as "black sheep of the family," "black lies," and the like.[6]

Whatever the criterion, the practice of maintaining chattel slaves persisted for generations. Principles of arbitrary rationale were evoked as circumstance saw fit and where ideological conditions were conducive. The African slave woman or man was considered private property, a possession of the white slaveholder.[7] Slave women and men had absolutely no human rights to which they could appeal. They were sold and purchased as chattel, often auctioned to the highest bidder. This web of oppression remained steadfast for over two centuries. Its legacy of violence fractured

---

5. Winthrop Jordan, *White Over Black* (Baltimore, Md.: Pelican, 1969), 73.

6. Ibid., 98.

7. See the excellent treatment of the origins of racism from a psycho-historical perspective, especially concerning the issue of property ownership which eventually became endemic to western European culture, in *White Racism: a Psycho-History* by Joel Kovel (New York: Columbia University Press, 1984), 21–22.

the fabric of family life of the African slave, as evident in the continued degeneration and rapid disintegration of the extended family concept that had prevailed in pre-slavery African culture, a disintegration now manifest in contemporary urban black family existence.

Particularly relevant to this study are religious developments that evolved during slavery's existence. Coupled with the disruption of the traditional cultural framework of the enslaved African and the brutalization of family separation were the severing of language ties and religious observances and practices. Forms of religious improvisation thus became normative as the Africans adopted the brand of Christianity imposed on them by their slavemasters and by itinerant missionary preachers. The plethora of European Christian denominations and ecclesiastical groupings were reflected in the slave community, but with certain modifications of European ritual to forms traditionally African. Baptist, Methodist, Episcopal, and Presbyterian denominations all had members who were slaves, with worship indigenized according to pre-slavery African customs and culture.[8]

The world of African culture, particularly its expression in worship, song, dance, and communal solidarity, was recreated within the slavery milieu by the African slave community.[9] It was, in fact, the distinctive form of the African experience of deity, together with the quest for total autonomy in religious life, that led to the formation of independent black churches. The first of these was a Baptist church founded in Silver Bluff, South Carolina, between 1773 and 1775.[10] During the final decades of the antebellum period, black Baptists, Methodists, and Presbyterians also constituted their own religious institutions, realizing that to function within the white religious community produced the inevitable white cultural, doctrinal, and social domination.[11]

Black slaves and white masters worshiped in the same locality, on the farms and plantations of white slaveholders, on Sunday mornings. But the black people often met secretly at night to engage in their own worship forms and to practice their private religious customs away from the watchful eye of slavemasters. These secret meetings represented the beginnings of the contemporary black church, sowing the seeds of the independent black church as we

---

8. John Blassingame, *Roll Jordan Roll: The World the Slaves Made* (New York: Pantheon Books, 1974), 115.

9. Ibid., 116–17.

10. Albert Raboteau, *Slave Religion* (New York: Oxford University Press, 1978), 139.

11. John Blassingame, *Roll Jordan Roll: The World the Slaves Made*, 119.

know it today.[12] The radical reinterpretation of the biblical narrative by the independent black church motivated many of its members to revolt against slavery, including in 1822 such notables as Morris Brown, assistant to church leader Nat Turner, and Denmark Vesey.[13] The character of the independent black Christian community provided fertile ground for radical black insurrectionists like Nat Turner, who lodged an armed rebellion in 1831, and for Frederick Douglass, an ex-slave and fierce lifetime abolitionist.

Slavery was still an accepted practice a year before the start of the Civil War. It had been adopted and affirmed by the United States Senate, in which the privileges and rights of slaveholders and property owners were vigorously championed.[14] The Republican party, which won the election in 1860, was constituted by both conservatives and radicals; the former were totally disinterested in the rights of black people, while the latter placed economic gain at the top of the agenda for their policy deliberations. The radicals, in fact, were unanimous in advocating freedom for the slaves — not for philanthropic reasons, but in order to facilitate the emergence of the growing industrialist capitalist class. The planter aristocracy was opposed to the expansion of northern capitalist interests.[15] President Lincoln made it clear that the salvation of the Union was primary and hence the freedom of the slaves was necessary for saving the nation. Ironically, black people who volunteered as soldiers in the Civil War were initially rejected by the white Union armies, who feared rebellion if blacks were armed. Toward the latter part of the Civil War, however, over two hundred thousand black soldiers were enlisted in the armed forces.[16] In a very real sense, the enslaved Africans who fought so valiantly "freed themselves during the Civil War."[17]

Emancipation and Exploitation

The "freed" African presented a problem to a society that enshrined racist values and refused to accord human rights to African and indigenous native peoples. To demonstrate their disapproval of "freed" Africans residing permanently in the United States, slaveholders formed the American Society for the Colonization of Free People of

---

12. Albert Raboteau, *Slave Religion*, 163.
13. Ibid.
14. E. Franklin Frazier, *The Negro in the United States* (New York: Macmillan, 1957), 103.
15. Ibid., 104.
16. Alphonso Pinkney, *Black Americans* (Englewood Cliffs, N.J.: Prentice Hall, 1975), 19.
17. Eric Foner, ed., *America's Black Past* (New York: Harper & Row, 1970), 241.

Color of the United States, which was responsible for the repatriation of Africans to places like Liberia and Sierra Leone in West Africa. Many whites could not conceive of a nonracist society in which blacks and whites were equal. Although Africans had shed their blood and sweat for generations to advance the course of western industrial civilization in the Americas, they were brutally excluded from participating in the sharing of its fruits. The African American scholar W. E. B. Du Bois lamented this anomaly of America's history in which Africans, together with peoples from the Americas and Asia, served as expendable appendages of labor and by force of racism laid the foundations of the contemporary unjust system of western European capitalism at the cost of the cheap labor of these peoples of color.[18]

Following emancipation, the rights of black people to acquire land in the southern states were severely curtailed by the Black Codes, which reflect the early statutes of apartheid in South Africa. Black people were also prohibited from possessing firearms to protect themselves against racist violence. President Andrew Johnson, in fact, vetoed the Congressional Civil Rights Act of 1866, but the Congress overrode his veto and extended citizenship rights to the black populace. Although the Fourteenth Amendment, which was promulgated in 1866 and subsequently ratified in 1868, sought to incriminate racial discrimination, there was still little protection against segregation of blacks in education, transportation, residence, and public utilities. The First Reconstruction Act legislated by Congress in 1867 affirmed the right of black males to vote in civil elections (all women were excluded from exercising this right), and state constitutions enabled the black community to seek the highest public office available to them, that of senator. Fourteen black men served in Congress within the House of Representatives between 1869 and the end of the Reconstruction period in 1877. Yet, unfortunately, because the primary interest of many of these elected officials was in their personal political prestige and the acquisition of social power, they disregarded the plight of the powerless black masses.

These black officials therefore generally served to legitimate white economic domination, which denied land ownership to black people in the South and prompted a mass exodus to the West.[19] The deprivation of a land base for blacks severely undermined the possibility of an independent economic base for the black community in the

18. W. E. B. Du Bois, *Black Reconstruction in America* (New York: Harcourt, Brace and Company, 1935), 15–16.

19. E. Franklin Frazier, *The Negro in the United States* (New York: Macmillan, 1957), 132.

United States.[20] By the early 1900s only a quarter of black people in the South lived on their own farms. The remaining three-quarters were reduced to the state of tenants and laborers on white farms. Most blacks became mired in debt as they endeavored to establish independent farms through borrowed capital for the purchase of farm equipment. Black people suffered economically in urban areas as well. The League for the Protection of Colored Women was formed in 1905 to aid poor and destitute black women in obtaining employment in large eastern cities like New York. Later, this organization, together with the Committee on Urban Conditions Among Negroes (designed to assist black people in coping with urban environments) came to be known as the National Urban League.[21]

Over time, the freed black population came to the realization that social mobility was possible only through educational achievement, a philosophy espoused by Booker T. Washington, the black leader renowned for his book, *Up From Slavery.* Numerous black aid societies and white philanthropists were instrumental in establishing several schools for black people in the northern and southern states.[22] The Freedmen's Bureau helped to finance institutions like Howard University, Atlanta University, Fisk University, Talladega College in Alabama, the Hampton Institute in Virginia, and many others. These prestigious black educational institutions were responsible for cultivating a tiny black educated elite in America which was bent on upward social mobility, not equality for all peoples. For the most part, this black elite ignored the growing black underclass developing beneath the white capitalist class. Likewise, the white philanthropic societies generally supported black industrial schools because they were opposed to integrated and equal education for blacks and whites.[23]

Amid the persistence of racism and exploitation of the labor of black people in the United States, a brilliant black social leader emerged in the early part of the twentieth century, W. E. B. Du Bois. Du Bois took issue with Booker T. Washington's approach of black accommodation to white supremacy and black striving to earn the respect of whites. Instead, he demanded that black people be accorded racial equality and social justice, and inaugurated the Niagara Movement to agitate for human rights for black people. He also served as editor of *Crisis* magazine and was a founder of

20. Rayford W. Logan, *The Negro in American Life and Thought: The Nadir, 1877–1901* (New York: The Dial Press, 1954), 123.
21. E. Franklin Frazier, *Black Bourgeoisie* (New York: The Free Press, 1965), 107.
22. August Meier and Elliott Rudwick, *From Plantation to Ghetto* (New York: Hill and Wang, 1966), 174.
23. E. Franklin Frazier, *Black Bourgeoisie* (New York: The Free Press, 1965), 150.

the National Association for the Advancement of Colored People (NAACP), which was organized in 1910 to promote and protect the equality of the rights of colored peoples in the United States as citizens of the United States.[24]

Du Bois maintained that a strong sense of unity and solidarity with Africans in Africa was essential for the struggle against European colonialism and racism. He contended that capitalism exploited Africans and other peoples of color for the accumulation of monetary wealth by the capitalist class. He was a prophet of great foresight when he criticized American society for its racism and economic injustice and for its concentration of the bulk of American political and economic power in the hands of a tiny white ruling elite. Du Bois' work through the NAACP was instrumental in confronting the mounting wave of legislation that enforced racial discrimination and segregation, carrying cases of civil rights violations of black people to the highest judicial level, the Supreme Court.

World War I saw the continuation of racism in all spheres of life in America, including within the armed forces. Both northern industrial cities and southern areas witnessed widespread terrorism against black people by groups like the Ku Klux Klan and the White Knights. These groups were violently committed to the principles of white supremacy and preserving sole white privilege. Scores of blacks were lynched by white mobs, leaving a trail of blood and death. Consequently, race riots flared as sprawling black communities ventilated their rage at racist violence — East St. Louis in 1917, Chicago in 1919, and Tulsa in 1921.

During the great depression of the late 1920s and early 1930s, blacks were driven into poverty at twice the rate of whites. At this time President Franklin Roosevelt inaugurated the historic New Deal that was designed to address the plight of the poor, and relief was provided to thousands of blacks trapped in the mire of poverty. Yet two years after the New Deal scheme, 3.5 million black people were still recipients of relief aid.[25] Clearly, fundamental economic and social issues facing black people were not addressed by the New Deal, which provided only temporary respite from racism and economic deprivation.

---

24. J. H. Franklin and Isidore Starr, *The Negro in 20th Century America* (New York: Vintage, 1967), 107.

25. Howard Zinn, ed., *New Deal Thought* (New York: The Bobbs-Merrill Co., Inc., 1966), 328.

The Struggle for Civil Rights

Several decades later, the protests against racism waged earlier by black people swelled into an unprecedented agitation for the enforcement of civil rights. Sparked by the refusal of a black woman, Rosa Parks, to surrender her bus seat to a white passenger in 1955, the Montgomery bus boycott was launched, growing into a movement of protests, boycotts, sit-ins, marches, and demonstrations in the demand for racial justice in America. Organizations like the Student Non-Violent Co-ordinating Committee (SNCC), the Congress on Racial Equality (CORE), and the Southern Christian Leadership Conference (SCLC) burgeoned in response to the crisis of black oppression.

The most prominent leader of this movement was Martin Luther King, Jr., a Baptist minister from Atlanta. King, together with various leaders within the Southern Christian Leadership Conference and black labor leaders — Bayard Rustin, Ralph Abernathy, A. Philip Randolph, Wyatt Tee Walker, Andrew Young, and Hosea Williams — helped to organize and coordinate the protests. The tactics employed were stringent non-cooperation with unjust and racist laws and a rigid adherence to nonviolent direct action. King, inspired by the black prophetic tradition derived from the era of antislavery and armed with the philosophy of *satyagraha* (truth-force) deployed by Gandhi in India as well as the teachings of Jesus reflected in the Sermon on the Mount, was adamant in his position that the entire civil rights movement be undergirded by the principle of nonviolence, and he repudiated any propensity toward militant self-defense.[26]

King's message mobilized millions of black, white, and other people of color in the struggle for freedom and dignity and ignited a movement for social justice and racial equality that became national in scope, sparking a crisis within white ruling circles, which few critics had anticipated. In 1963, for example, the famous March on Washington gathered two hundred fifty thousand people of all races in the nation's capital to demand racial justice, political freedom, jobs, and the passage of the Civil Rights Bill. King's galvanizing of black people across the country through protracted protests, persistent marches, escalating sit-ins, and demonstrations came to constitute what is known today as the civil rights movement.

President John F. Kennedy, although supportive of this civil rights movement, nevertheless made a massive blunder by allow-

---

26. M. L. King, *Stride Toward Freedom* (New York: Harper & Brothers, 1958), 177–78.

ing the southern states to appoint judges to federal courts. As the black community turned to litigation to counter the evil of segregation by taking numerous institutions to the courts in the bid to win justice, the result was often the rancor of racism and the cancer of segregation. Despite racism within the judicial system, however, the civil rights movement was successful in contributing major victories for institutionalized racial equality, such as the desegregation of schools through Supreme Court decisions like *Brown v. Board of Education* in 1954, and the passage of the Civil Rights Bill in 1965. King's nonviolent crusade for social and economic justice, however, was short-lived. He was assassinated on April 15, 1968, while the United States of America was still clearly in disharmony with King's chord of racial harmony and social justice for all of its citizens.

Not all voices within the civil rights movement reflected the moderation exhibited by Martin Luther King, Jr. Between 1964 and 1966, numerous splits occurred within the civil rights movement that King had initially led. Black radicalism was on the rise, especially among black youth, who refused any level of compromise with white America. The outbreak of the Vietnam war and America's massive military and political involvement exacerbated the existing ideological lines of division. King had prophetically criticized America's role in Vietnam, a denunciation that had earned him the criticism of groups like the NAACP and the Urban League, whose leaders did not recognize the interrelationship between America's militaristic policy abroad and its practices of racism domestically.

One of those dissenting voices within the civil rights movement was that of Malcolm X, the black Muslim leader. Malcolm X perceived the teachings of King on nonviolence to be unrealistic in the context of repression imposed by the United States and its military agencies. He advocated black nationalism, maintaining that liberation of black people was justified "by any means necessary." He analyzed the situation of black people in America as one of internal colonialism and defended the right of black people to protect themselves against racist violence by force if necessary, because of the violence of America's social and economic structures against blacks. He extolled the principle of black self-love in a land where blackness was denigrated, and called for the unity of the black nation in America. Malcolm X contended that independence and separation from white racist society was the principal means by which black people would be free, and his fiery speeches and militant rhetoric appealed to the millions of black people disenfranchised and disinherited in America's northern industrial ghettoes.

Malcolm X met with violent opposition to his message, and

was assassinated on February 21, 1965, three years before King's death. He left the legacy of his Organization of Afro-American Unity, which was geared toward unifying black people in the United States and in Africa in order to enhance black political cohesion. The following year, H. Rap Brown of SNCC coined the term "Black Power" at a civil rights rally in Mississippi. Other black nationalist organizations began to emerge, all expressing the objectives of black self-determination and aspiring toward black national independence. These groups were championed by persons like Stokely Carmichael (now Kwame Toure) of SNCC and Black Panther Party members Eldridge Cleaver and Huey Newton.

Yet despite the appeal of the message of black independence and the legislative successes of the civil rights movement in the sixties, social and economic statistics from the seventies reveal how far the nation was from true equality among races. During the seventies massive numbers of black people from rural areas moved into the northern and southern cities. New York's black population increased by 290,000, Detroit's by 178,000, Washington, D.C.'s by 126,000, Houston's by 102,000, and Atlanta's by 69,000.[27] Two-thirds of the black population lived in the sixty-seven largest metropolitan areas. This influx provoked an efflux of whites to the outer suburbs, appropriately termed "white flight." Residential segregation persisted, with most black people living in the inner cities and only a tiny percentage possessing the material resources necessary to move to suburban areas. The black ghettoes of the inner cities represent the legacy of racism and exclusivism: a consistent refusal to grant equal housing, education, and economic and political rights to black people and a denial of any genuine form of the racial integration and community harmony that blacks may have initially hoped for and thought possible.

The Reagan Era

During the eighties, with Ronald Reagan as president, black people were particularly victimized by the accentuation of free market philosophy and expansion of supply side economics. Their social powerlessness and economic deprivation reached catastrophic proportions, a fact that is substantiated by numerous statistics from social and research agencies.[28] Even though candidate Ronald Reagan included within his litany of promises the commitment to

---

27. Ibid., 316.
28. See Appendix B.

"improve and defend"[29] historical black colleges and other educational institutions, the effects of his policies upon taking office in 1981 were diametrically opposed to these goals. Reagan's budget reduced funding for public education, severely attacked social programs, and lacerated affirmative action and job training programs that were of vital assistance to poor people.

The attitude reflected by the Reagan regime was one of tolerance and protectionism of racism, encouraging the already existing racially discriminatory social character of American society. Quotas for black faculty and students at white universities were revoked and black educators studying for their doctorates in education were warned of having their junior faculty status nullified should they be unable to complete their studies by November 30, 1981.[30] Reagan's administration reversed many possible gains for black people socially and educationally, especially by underfunding historical black colleges and generally cutting back on financing public institutions of higher learning upon which the majority of black people depend for their education.

Statistics from the eighties indicate little improvement from the seventies; in fact, in some areas conditions worsened.[31] In places like New York City, the most heavily populated city in the United States, three-quarters of black people and eighty percent of Latinos dropped out or did not graduate in four years.[32] Within the penal system, over one million people were incarcerated in America's jails, and fifty percent of them were black. (This incarceration rate of two hundred fifty per one hundred thousand exceeded that of the racist state of South Africa.) Close to fifty black men were hanged in cells throughout the United States in 1981 alone, with the authorities claiming "suicide" as the cause of death.[33] Violence against black students in 1981 continued throughout the decade on university campuses across the country. Morgan State University in Baltimore, Wesleyan College in Connecticut, Amherst College in Massachusetts, and Stanford University in California were all scenes of racist slogans and nasty epithets hurled at black students. These incidents evoke pictures of the days of slavery when black people were subject to beatings, whippings, lynchings, and floggings by southern white slaveholders. Responses to police violence against black people have also precipitated outbursts of anger

---

29. Manning Marable, *How Capitalism Underdeveloped Black America*, (Boston: South End Press, 1984), 222.
30. Ibid., 226.
31. See Appendix B.
32. *Peoples Daily World* newspaper, October 26, 1988, 5.
33. See Appendix B.

on the part of the black community, triggering such rebellions as that provoked by the jury verdict in April 1992 after the Rodney King beating in Los Angeles, California.[34]

What needs to be underscored in the context of the eighties and nineties is the devastating effect that Reagan's election of 1980 and his reelection of 1984 had on the social and economic fabric of the black community, particularly among the black working class and underclass. For example, in 1981 alone, the average income among black people dropped by 5.2 percent.[35] The effects of the Reagan policies were more clearly indicated in the rapid disintegration of black community life: unusually high unemployment, a preposterous incarceration rate of black men, excessively large drop-out rates of black school children, fragmentation of the black family unit, soaring infant mortality rates, and the escalating descent of unprecedented numbers of black people into the abyss of poverty.[36] Despite certain gains and advances in civil rights legislation in the sixties, events of the following decades indicate that America's economic creed of capitalism and its practice of racism in the nineties continues to undermine racial equality.[37]

---

34. For details of responses of black outrage over racist acts, see Rod Bush (ed.), *The New Black Vote* (San Francisco: Synthesis Publications, 1984), 7. Rodney King, a black man was severely beaten by police officers in Los Angeles in early 1991. Though the beating was videotaped, the jury verdict in the case acquitted the police officers who brutalized King, sparking the most inflammatory uprising in Los Angeles' history. Only after a federal re-trial in early 1993 were two of the four officers charged found guilty.

35. Manning Marable, *Black American Politics* (London: Verso, 1985), 104.

36. Ibid. The following statistics underscore the magnitude of the effects of Reagan's policies of racism on black people generally:

By 1982, 20% of all black males of working age, about 2 million persons were out of the labor force, a 300% increase since 1960. Black young adults experienced official employment rates of about 50% in 1982–83 and unofficial rates in many ghettoes exceeded 80%. The impact upon black families was inevitable. The proportion of two parent black families dropped to 53%; over half of all Afro-American children were born out of wedlock in the mid 1980s. Since 1960 the number of Afro-American families headed by single, divorced or widowed women had increased by over 30% and more than 60% of these families lived in poverty. Overall, black median families' income in 1983 had fallen to only 55% of white family income — the largest wage gap recorded in a quarter of a century. More than half of all black children under the age of three in 1983 were living in poverty. . . . Black male teenagers were admitted to state and county mental hospitals at a rate two and a half times that of white male teenagers. For black males aged 25–44, the rate of mental hospital admissions was almost three times higher than that for white males in 1980. . . . Approximately 300,000 Afro-Americans were incarcerated by 1983, most of whom were under thirty years of age. (cited in Marable, 104)

37. See Appendix C.

South Africa: Racism Enshrined in the State

I have cherished the ideal of a democratic and free society in which all persons live together in harmony and with equal opportunities. It is an ideal which I hope to live for and to achieve. But if needs be, it is an ideal for which I am prepared to die.

—*Nelson Mandela, No Easy Walk to Freedom*

Prior to the European intrusion into southern Africa in 1652, the aboriginal inhabitants of that region of the subcontinent possessed a sophisticated civilization characterized by flourishing schemes of agriculture, invention of metal implements, trade with neighboring nations, and a high level of cultural solidarity and social stability.[38] The indigenous peoples of the Cape region were the Khoi Khoi on the southeastern tip and the San on the southwestern side of southern Africa. In the inland areas and along the southern and eastern coastlines lived the Zulu and the Xhosa-speaking people, descendants of the Nguni nation.

Marked similarities among the various nations of southern Africa were reflected in the closeness of cultural and linguistic patterns. Fraternal ties existed among the diverse groups who gathered in clans and villages. Contrary to the distorted view of some historians that indigenous Africans were war-mongering people, feuding and internecine hostilities were rare. The existence of an ethos of harmony and stability is supported by anthropological and historical evidence of the French scholar Jean Hiernaux.[39] Such facts contradict the generally held white South African historical perception that the African people were bent on destroying themselves until Europeans benevolently rescued them from certain death. The historical evidence is clear that the violence of apartheid dispossession is essentially responsible for the chaos in South Africa today, not the "black on black" violence that is widely held to be the primary cause of instability in the country.

Colonialism and the Institutionalization of Racism

The indigenous people of the southwestern region of South Africa, namely, the Khoi Khoi, the San, and the Xhosa nations, were ini-

---

38. There is evidence to suggest that there was an Iron Age among Sotho-speaking people in the fifth century A.D. See Leonard Thompson, ed., *African Societies in Southern Africa* (New York: Praeger, 1969), 6–9.

39. See the appendix of the author's M.A. thesis, Pacific School of Religion, 1984, "Black Theology and Liberation Praxis in South Africa (Azania)" available at the Graduate Theological Union library, Berkeley, California, for a detailed treatment of the history of the peoples of South Africa.

tially hospitable to the European visitors, accepting them as foreign explorers on African territory. The African people demonstrated an openness to the strangers with little suspicion on first contact. Their attitude gradually changed, however, when they learned that the Europeans were intent on pillaging African lands and abusing the hospitality of their hosts. The Dutch settlers, for example, began encroaching on farmland belonging to the African people. A series of wars (1659, during the 1770s, 1846, and 1850-1853) were consequently waged by the Khoi Khoi, San, and Xhosa nations in defense of their lands. These communities refused to acquiesce to the onslaught of the Dutch invaders.

The British arrived at the Cape in 1806 and subsequently colonized it as an extension of their colonialist-imperialist program in Africa and the world. The Dutch decided that they could not live under the colonial domination of the British, and thus ventured into the interior of the country in pursuit of more fertile lands, such as Natal and the Transvaal, where they inevitably encountered other indigenous Sotho- and Zulu-speaking people. Through continued military conquests and the use of firearms, the Europeans eventually dispossessed the indigenous black people of their land. The African nations, however, were not prepared to capitulate to the theft of their lands by white settlers and consistently waged wars of attrition to preserve their land base.

December 18, 1838 stands as a catastrophic day in the life of the southern African peoples. Hundreds of black people were massacred on this day by the firepower of the Dutch settler colonialists in a fierce war to retain African ancestral lands. A river located close to this carnage became known as Blood River because it flowed red with the blood of Africans slain during battle. The Afrikaner Boers, on the other hand, erected the Voortrekker Hoogte Monument to celebrate the day and to symbolize their gratitude to their God. This monument is still acclaimed by many white Afrikaners in South Africa today.

Despite the massacre, however, the indigenous African people continued to resist the escalating encroachment on their land. They were victorious on occasion, notwithstanding the heavy artillery of the British, as at Isandlwana in 1853 under the command of Cetshwayo. It was only through the continuous infusion and utility of heavy arms that the Europeans, consisting of the combined forces of the British and the Dutch, were able to finally conquer the indigenous people after a series of wars toward the end of the nineteenth century. The African people had persevered in ceaseless resistance prior to their final defeat.

The Response to European Missionary Endeavors

During the seventeenth century, the Dutch Reformed Church was established at the Cape as part of the Dutch East India Company's attempt to settle Dutch citizens there. It is interesting to note that though the Dutch Reformed Church baptized children of those black people who were forcibly enslaved by the Dutch, historical baptismal registers in Cape Town do not include children of interracial black-white parentage. The seal of Christian baptism evidently did not imply freedom for slaves, nor the according of human rights to interracial children, since the church viewed such offspring as "illegitimate."[40]

In the nineteenth century, as the Puritan and Pietist religious movements in England and Germany expanded, missionaries from these nations came to South Africa to fulfil what they perceived to be their responsibility of bringing the Christian gospel to the "heathen." Methodist missionaries from England arrived in 1816, followed by the Presbyterians of the Glasgow Missionary Society in 1821 and the Moravians and Lutherans in the 1830s. While the colonists were preoccupied with dispossessing the African people of their lands, the churches were generally involved in the task of indoctrinating the indigenous people with the ideology of passivity and acceptance of their subjugation.[41]

Black Christians decided to break away from the European mission churches and form their own indigenous, independent churches, including the African Methodist Episcopal Church, the Ethiopian churches under the leadership of Mangena Mokone in the 1890s, the African Presbyterian Churches led by P. J. Mzimba, the Nazarite churches inspired by Isaiah Shembe in 1898, and the Christian Apostolic Zionist Churches formed in 1904. For the first time these African Christians were able to express their faith free of missionary tutelage and the pervasiveness of racism in the mission churches.[42]

---

40. Jonathan Gerstner, "The Thousand Generation Covenant: Dutch Reformed Covenant Theology and the Colonists of South Africa," unpublished Ph.D. dissertation, 366.

41. Louise Stack and Don Morton make the point that "the churches' betrayal of the Gospel begins with the condoning of slaves, the warring crusades and the preachers of colonialism. . . . While the colonialists were busy robbing the people of their land in Southern Africa, the church was right alongside, giving its blessing." Cited in *Torment to Triumph in Southern Africa* (New York: Friendship Press, 1976), 47.

42. For a more detailed elaboration on the history and formation of the indigenous churches, see Bengt Sundkler, *Bantu Prophets in South Africa* (Oxford: Oxford University Press, 1961)

The Epoch of Nonviolent Resistance

In 1906 a prominent leader named Bambhata organized a protest against the introduction of a land tax foisted on Africans by the British. The British responded to the nonviolent protest by cruelly executing Bambhata and brutalizing the protesters. This event signified the first act of military violence against the people of South Africa in the twentieth century. Following the white-led formation of four provinces into the Union of South Africa in 1910, in which the British government officially ceded South Africa to the white settlers, the establishment of white power in South Africa was virtually complete. As a consequence, the African National Congress took form in 1912, to wage the struggle for black freedom. The following year, the colonial regime promulgated the Native Land Act, which stipulated that blacks could only purchase certain tracts of land confined to seven percent of South Africa's total land area. This law marked the beginning of the dispossession of the African people in the twentieth century.

Other laws restricting black people's movement and rights were also instituted, especially laws affecting workers. In May 1918, sanitation workers in Johannesburg went on strike, resulting in the incarceration of 152 persons, while scores of others were sentenced to two months of hard labor. In 1920, African miners went on strike for decent earnings. The police opened fire on the strikers, killing eleven and wounding many others. In 1921, over forty thousand health education workers demonstrated for higher wages. Again the regime responded to the demonstration with brute force, gunning down forty of the workers.

Peaceful protests continued through 1927 and 1928, with dock workers and diamond miners demonstrating against reductions of already sub-minimum wages. The police again resorted to armed force to suppress the demonstration, injuring many. Similarly, in 1929, police bullets felled African protesters for demanding the abolition of the notorious passbook law. This law required that all Africans carry a book of identification on their person at all times, as part of the regime's measure to control the movement of black people. Failure to produce the passbook on demand by a policeman resulted in imprisonment with hard labor.

Widespread and sustained protests persisted over the next two decades, with each protest utilizing nonviolent or passive resistance methods. In 1942 and 1944, municipal workers and railway laborers in the Johannesburg area struck for more livable wages. Sixteen persons were shot at point blank range in one incident alone. In 1946, when African mineworkers (the sector that produces the bulk of South Africa's industrial wealth) went on strike, armed police forced workers to return to work at gun point.

In 1948, the Nationalist party, elected solely by white voters, came to power. It basically predicated many of its policies on principles derived from Hitler's Nazi Germany, since the latter served as a source of inspiration to the white nationalists. Their formation of the apartheid charter institutionalized racism, defining all areas of civil life in South Africa according to race. A host of repressive and restrictive laws for blacks were instituted thereafter, including the Group Areas Act in 1950, which confined black people to certain residential areas only — the most barren areas of the country; the Suppression of Communism and Terrorism Acts in 1950, which made any person voicing views against the state liable for imprisonment for up to life; and the Bantu Education Act in 1953, which proposed an inferior type of education for black people designed to produce persons who would serve the white economy.

Nonviolent protests against these repressive laws gathered widespread support among black people. In 1958, thousands of black women marched on the capital city of Pretoria to protest the law requiring passbooks for women similar to those carried by black men. The police beat and injured several of the protesting women. The incident which caused the greatest shock in South Africa occurred at Sharpeville, outside Johannesburg, on March 21, 1960. Sixty-nine people were killed and one hundred eighty-eight were wounded for burning their passbooks in protest against the governmental law requiring such humiliating documents. The protest was organized by the Pan Africanist Congress of Azania, an Africanist group that had split from the African National Congress in 1959. This historic event marked a watershed in the course of the South African struggle. Black people came to the painful realization that peaceful protest in South Africa was futile and even suicidal. Other avenues of struggle had to be explored because the white state had closed its doors to the possibility of a peaceful, nonviolent, negotiated settlement of the South African crisis.

Armed Struggle and the Philosophy
of Black Consciousness

After the historic Sharpeville incident the black liberation movements — the African National Congress (ANC) and the Pan Africanist Congress (PAC) — were declared illegal by the state and consequently forced underground. At this juncture these organizations conceded that the last remaining recourse for resistance to the apartheid machine was that of armed struggle. The ANC and

PAC organized military wings with a specific campaign of limited guerilla warfare directed toward military targets and other strategic symbols of the apartheid apparatus.

In 1961, several leaders of the ANC were arrested and sentenced to life imprisonment in the famous Treason Trial, which lasted a number of years. The state tried several leaders of the Defiance Campaign, which called for massive disobedience to South Africa's racist laws, and found them guilty of treason and threatening to overthrow the state through force. These African leaders, including Nelson Mandela and Walter Sisulu, were banished to Robben Island in 1964 for their participation in resistance activities.

The late sixties and seventies were marked by the emergence of the Black Consciousness Movement inaugurated by Steven Biko. Organizations such as the South African Students Organization (SASO) and the Black People's Convention (BPC) were formed to draw together various sectors of the black population. Raising consciousness was a key component of the Black Consciousness Movement, and the movement brought about massive strikes, boycotts, and demonstrations throughout the country in defiance of the apartheid state. The philosophy of black consciousness taught black pride and self-esteem and the awareness that black people had to free themselves from psychic enslavement by white racism in order to liberate the oppressed South African nation.

June 16, 1976 heralded yet another turning point in the South African freedom struggle. In that year thousands of black students demonstrated against the notorious Bantu Education system in the township of Soweto outside Johannesburg. The Bantu Education Act of 1953 had created an inferior and racist educational system intended to prepare black students for menial labor positions in the white controlled economy, with emphasis on subjects like domestic science to equip black women for servant roles in white households.[43] Other notable features included overcrowded classrooms, underqualified teachers, and poorly equipped school facilities.[44] Although the students were waging a peaceful demonstration, the regime responded with massive brute force and heavy military artillery. In a carnage that is still widely commemorated in South Africa and throughout the world, over a thousand students were

---

43. This system of indoctrination is well described in the BBC film documentary, *Six Days in Soweto*, made in 1977. It is available from the Southern African Media Center in San Francisco.

44. See for instance Eric Molobi, "From Bantu Education to People's Education" in *Popular Struggles in South Africa*, ed. W. Cobbett and R. Cohen (Trenton: Africa World Press with James Currey, London, 1988), for a summation of the dimensions of Bantu Education and the need for its transformation.

brutally gunned down by police, the youngest being thirteen-year-old Hector Pieterson. Thousands of students consequently had to flee the country for fear of being arrested or killed by police. Many joined the ranks of the exiled liberation movements to intensify the struggle against the apartheid regime.

And the violence continued. September through October of 1977 witnessed a series of tragedies and the compounding of oppressive legislation, banning almost all major black political organizations. Steven Biko, the leader of the Black Consciousness Movement, was callously killed by police on September 12, 1977, an incident about which the minister of justice, Jimmy Kruger, remarked "His death leaves me cold." In the face of rising opposition, the racist regime was demonstrating an unconscionable desperation to suppress black dissent to white domination.

Undeterred by the violence, black people intensified their struggle against apartheid in the eighties. A black trade union movement emerged in various parts of South Africa and the mobilization of various sectors of the black student community began in 1980. These organizations asserted the rights of black workers in the industrial arenas that had been exploited by capitalist economic practices such as cheap labor rates. The unjust educational system for black people was vigorously opposed by thousands of students who launched protracted boycotts of classes. In June 1980, twenty-five people were killed by police in Elsies River outside Cape Town for protesting against racist policies in education and employment.

In 1983, two sectors within the black community that the white minority regime had attempted to co-opt into a tricameral white-run parliament (the "colored" and "Indian" populations) overwhelmingly rejected this effort to entrench apartheid further. Less than twenty percent of these sectors participated in these farcical elections. Similarly, too, with the formation of the regional services councils among the urban African community, a policy whereby local black officials were given the responsibility of managing apartheid, eighty percent of black township residents across the country (including ninety percent of the residents of Soweto, the country's largest township) boycotted these bogus structures.[45] Numerous persons who opted to participate in this political charade were either assassinated or forced to resign after realizing that the black community did not view collaborators with apartheid amicably. Young black activists therefore established independent political structures and educational cells within the black townships to raise the conscious-

---

45. Stanley Greenberg, "Resistance and Hegemony" in *The State of Apartheid*, ed. W. G. James (Boulder, Colo.: Lynne Rienner Publishers, 1987), 54.

ness of the black masses. For months, thousands of black residents living in the townships of the Transvaal and Cape Provinces refused to pay rents on their homes to the authorities and resisted the imposition of rent increases. As part of the strategy of resistance and noncooperation with apartheid capitalists, the Port Elizabeth area in the Cape Province initiated a series of boycotts of white stores by black consumers. This precipitated the closure of many white stores, whose owners complained directly to white president P. W. Botha.

During the mid-eighties, the black townships and ghettoes, where police repression was the order of the day, were transformed into training areas for political revolution and organized mass resistance. On July 20, 1985, a national state of emergency was invoked in response to the escalating black revolt, affecting thirty-six magisterial districts in the country. This announcement allowed the military sector of South Africa to execute necessary action to contain the flames of the widescale dissent engulfing the black townships. More than fifty thousand police and security personnel were involved in the military clampdown on the black community. Military anti-riot trucks and armored carriers manned by soldiers were stationed permanently in several black communities, and in many townships, including Soweto, Sebokeng, Kattlehong, and Boiphatong in the Vaal Triangle, and Zwide and Langa in the Cape. Military authorities intimidated, arrested, tortured, and imprisoned thousands of black women, men, and children who were thought to be responsible for the swelling agitation. In one incident alone, over eight hundred children between the ages of nine and fifteen were arrested and held by the military. By the end of 1985, government figures cited the killing of 763 people by the police "of whom only three were white and 201 were children"; in addition, 2,571 had been shot and wounded.[46] By the end of 1985, over twenty thousand people had been either arrested or detained by the authorities. Scores of black activists disappeared without a trace. Hundreds of children were detained and held incommunicado in indoctrination detention camps.

In November 1985, the Congress of South African Trade Unions (COSATU) was formed, representing some five hundred thousand black workers at that time and currently estimated to have a membership of 1.5 million people with over 300 unions affiliated to the coalition. This worker organization, together with two other major trade union coalitions, the National Council of Trade Unions (NACTU) and the Azanian Workers Union (AZAWU), as well as

---

46. Anthony Sampson, *Black and Gold* (New York: Pantheon Books, 1987), 182.

two political organizations, the United Democratic Front (UDF), a broadbased resistance organization, and the National Forum (NF), a black consciousness grouping, mobilized 1.5 million black workers on May 1, 1986, in one of the largest worker strikes in South African history. A similar action occurred on the tenth anniversary of the Soweto uprising on June 16. In October 1986, the National Union of Mineworkers, representing some five hundred thousand black miners in the gold, coal, and diamond mines of South Africa, launched an unprecedented three-week strike to demand livable wages and decent working and living conditions. Despite the refusal by the mining industrial establishment to concede to their demands, the workers demonstrated the power of their labor muscle. Over $100 million in production costs were lost by the mining conglomerates because of the strike. Black miners, the workers at the lowest end of the worker continuum, had made it dramatically clear that they were prepared to pay the ultimate price for economic justice and political liberation in South Africa: to sacrifice their livelihood and remittances for their poverty-stricken families, and to face the reality of physical starvation and military terror.

According to reports of the Detainees Parents Support Committee, almost nine thousand children were still being held in detention by the end of 1986.[47] From September of 1985 to August of 1987, two thousand persons had been killed and nineteen thousand had been arrested or detained.[48] One hundred and eighty people had been killed by the end of 1987.[49] In the eighties over thirty-three black schools were closed in the Eastern Cape and many more in the Transvaal area.

The situation around the Pietermaritzburg area of Natal province deteriorated into one of internecine conflict, as tensions between Inkatha, led by white government appointee Chief Gatsha Buthelezi, and the United Democratic Front (UDF) surfaced. Buthelezi's status as Kwazulu "Bantustan" leader made him a consistent target of the black resistance. The Bantustans were scattered and unproductive pieces of land that constituted thirteen percent of South Africa's total land area and were set aside under apartheid for the eighty-five percent black majority. The Bantustans represented internal structures of apartheid, and most black people viewed and continue to view Buthelezi as a collaborator with apartheid by legitimating the regime's "tribalistic" divisions of black people, which facilitated the ancient colonial policy of "divide and rule."

---

47. *Africa News*, 29. 1 (June 11, 1988): 13.
48. Anthony Sampson, *Black and Gold* (New York: Pantheon, 1987), 73.
49. *Africa News*, 28. 5 (November 16, 1987): 2.

Meanwhile, white authorities proceeded with their policy of the Bantustans, forcibly dislocating 3.5 million black people from their ancestral lands and relocating them into arid reserves akin to those of the indigenous Indian reservations in the United States. In May 1986, more than thirty thousand black people were forced to flee their homes in Crossroads, a slum settlement outside metropolitan Cape Town that had been established by women who insisted on living together with their husbands, who were migrant workers from the countryside. In August 1988, over five thousand people had their squatter shacks razed to the ground at Emzomusha (Love Zone) outside Durban in Natal province, the area earmarked for white property development.[50] An estimated seven million black people remain homeless in South Africa, half of them in Natal and the rest in the Witwatersrand and Cape regions — an ironic statistic in a country where a surplus of forty-five thousand houses in white areas have been left vacant for lack of white occupants.

The history of the South African struggle took a new turn in March 1990, due to the pressure from protracted internal black resistance and the impact of international economic sanctions against the apartheid regime. Previously banned organizations like the ANC, the PAC, and the South African Communist Party (SACP), were unbanned, and Nelson Mandela and several other imprisoned black leaders were released. Thus began the era of negotiations in which the ANC and the white government, led by F. W. De Klerk, committed themselves to a peaceful settlement of the South African conflict, so that there can be a negotiated transition toward majority rule under the auspices of the Conference for a Democratic South Africa (CODESSA). These negotiations have culminated in national elections planned for April 26–28, 1994. Tragically, the issues of the white minority monopoly of ownership of 87% of South Africa's land and 70% of the country's wealth, and black people's poverty, homelessness and landlessness are still unaddressed, and will remain so following the country's apartheid orchestrated elections. White power in South Africa reigns supreme, conveying the impression of conceding political power to black people while essentially retaining economic power.

---

50. *City Press*, Johannesburg, August 28, 1988.

Racism in the United States and South Africa

In many ways, there are closer parallels between the history of the indigenous Indians of North America and the black people of South Africa than between the history of black people in these countries,[51] but there are strikingly similar patterns in the resistance of black people in the United States and South Africa against racism. These patterns of resistance include protracted protests, demonstrations, boycotts, worker strikes, development of community self-defense units, black consciousness militance, armed struggle, and grass-roots organizing for self-determination, though there are also some significant differences owing to the variances of location and circumstances in both struggles. One such difference is that black people were brought to the United States from Africa to work as slave labor in the cotton plantations in an alien land and were thus stripped of their language and heritage; in South Africa, Africans were forced to work in South African gold and diamond mines and were thus enslaved in their own country. Secondly, in the United States black people remain a numerical minority of the population, whereas in South Africa, black people have always been the overwhelming majority, with a current population exceeding that of the white minority by six times.

A third difference in the circumstances in which resistance to racism emerged is that the Constitution of the United States serves as the basis for administering racial equality, although the document originally excluded the indigenous Native Americans, Africans, women, and all persons not possessing property, whereas in South Africa the constitutional provision that exists is the apartheid charter, which denies fundamental rights to all black people.[52]

---

51. An excellent text that confirms these parallels is the recent publication, *The State of Native America: Genocide, Colonization and Resistance,* ed. Annette Jaimes (Boston: South End Press, 1992). This work delineates in comprehensive detail with extensive footnotes the various aspects of indigenous Indian experience, illuminating such issues as history, self-determination and sovereignty, education, treaty rights, water rights, religious rights, fishing rights, political prisoners, native American women, environmental contamination, and the military. W. M. Tsotsi's *From Chattel to Wage Slavery* (Maseru: Lesotho Printing and Publishing, 1981), furnishes a detailed treatment of the struggle against racism and colonization from the seventeenth century to the late 1970s waged by the black people of South Africa.

52. It was only in late 1993 that a new "post-apartheid" constitution was agreed upon by the various political parties participating in the Kempton Park negotiation talks. However, it needs to be pointed out that the body that drew up the new constitution did not have a mandate from the people of South Africa to engage in such serious political deliberations. There was no formal consultation with the black majority in the launching of the negotiation process, making the constitution

Fourthly, though black people in the United States have experienced the ravages of racist segregation under Jim Crow laws in this century, no people in the world have been singularly victimized by the totalitarian racially oppressive system of apartheid as have the black people of South Africa. A fifth difference is that the black struggle of the twentieth century in the United States has generally functioned within the limits of the political and social system, with the exception of black nationalist movements like that of Marcus Garvey's Universal Negro Improvement Association of the 1920s and Malcolm X's Black Muslims Incorporated of the sixties, while much of the black struggle in South Africa has focused on overthrowing the system of apartheid by armed struggle if need be.

A final difference in circumstances is that the black struggle in the United States has generally not been an anti-capitalist one, with the exception of radical black organizations such as the All African Peoples' Revolutionary Party, the former Black Panthers, the African Peoples' Socialist Party, and the Republic of New Afrika, to name a few, whereas in the South African situation, strong anti-capitalist sentiments are expressed by almost all of the principal liberation movements, at least at their inception.

Though there are differences in the histories of black people's struggles in the United States and South Africa, both have a common denominator: the attempt of black people to be human on their own terms, free from the yoke of racial oppression and the manacles of economic servitude. Fortunately, these struggles for humanity and restoration persist and inevitably strike a strong theological chord within the orchestra of creation. Such struggles also have much to do with understanding the Word of the Creator amid the travail of black humanity. In the next chapter we will consider responses from two black theologians to the question of racial oppression, James Cone and Desmond Tutu, as a precursor to our final thesis that black theological responses to such questions warrant serious and detailed social analysis for the purpose of reconstructing positive, nonracist, democratic, and liberated societies in the United States and South Africa.

---

flawed at its foundations. Further, the new constitution protects white property and landowners, with no provisions for fundamental redistribution of South Africa's land and wealth.

Chapter 2

The Theologies of James Cone
and Desmond Tutu

Black theologians feel the need to show the liberating character of black Christianity in our struggle for social and political justice. But in our effort to show that the gospel is political, we are sometimes in danger of reducing black worship to a political strategy session, thereby distorting the essence of black religion.

—*James Cone*[1]

If it weren't for faith, I would have given up long ago. I am certain lots of us would have been hate-filled and bitter. For me the Scriptures have become more and more thoroughly relevant to our situation. They speak of a God who, when you worship him, turns you around to be concerned for your neighbor. He does not tolerate a relationship with himself that excludes your neighbor.... In the middle of our faith is the death and resurrection. Nothing could have been more hopeless than Good Friday—but then Easter happened and forever we have been prisoners of hope.

—*Desmond Tutu*[2]

The fact that racism is a global phenomenon requires that scholars throughout the world pool their creative intellectual resources in the struggle to eliminate this scourge on our society. Theologians especially are called to this task of addressing racial injustice, for is not all humankind, indeed all creation, created by the Creator? James Cone from the African American context and Desmond

1. James Cone, "Sanctification and Liberation in the Black Religious Tradition" in *Sanctification and Liberation*, ed. Theodore Runyon (Nashville: Abingdon Press, 1981), 174.
2. Desmond Tutu, "Prisoners of Hope," *Sojourners* (February 1985): 24.

Tutu from the South African context have devoted their lives and work to the eradication of racism in their respective situations. While Cone and Tutu have given much thought to the problem, they are, most importantly, conscious also of the social and economic factors underlying racist oppression. Their interdisciplinary theological methodologies thus provide a vital perspective on how to intensify the struggle against racism, classism, sexism, and economic exploitation in the United States and South Africa.

James Cone

Social Analysis and Black Theology

James Cone continues to focus on the need for social analysis in black theology. He argues that the lack of its use during the sixties resulted in a weak and inadequate response to racist oppression in the United States. He contends that social analysis is imperative for all liberation theologies, especially since liberation theologies are directly related to the concrete and practical struggles of the poor and oppressed.[3] Precisely for this reason Cone's thinking in the area of black theology and social analysis method in theology provide fertile ground for a deeper probing of the persistence of racism as a means of proposing possible modes of redressing the problem of its existence.

Cone recognizes the current deficiencies of black theology and displays an openness to external criticism while acknowledging the need for constant internal criticism. He contends that the utility of social analysis is a second element of black theological method: "Racism, sexism, capitalism, and militarism must be comprehensively analyzed so that these demons can be destroyed."[4] According to Cone, the failure of many black theologians to engage in earnest economic and social analysis has resulted in a simplistic conceptualization of and unsophisticated response to the tenacity of racism. He contends that moral persuasion is inadequate as a weapon in the struggle against racism and that the "tools of the social sciences" are indispensable to this movement of liberation.[5]

The principal reason for the vital omission of social analysis in black theology, Cone surmises, is the middle-class origins and reactionary posture of many black theologians and clergypersons.

---

3. James Cone, "The Gospel and the Liberation of the Poor" in *Christian Century* 98 (February 18, 1981): 107.
4. James Cone, *For My People* (Maryknoll, N.Y: Orbis Books, 1984), 151–52.
5. Ibid., 88.

Instead of being proactive in a program of black liberation, they, for the most part, remained reactive to the actions of white society. Cone is therefore concerned that the black middle class has benefited from the civil rights movement of the sixties, while the plight of the black poor continues to be largely ignored by mainstream American society.[6] Many black organizations have continued to depend on white churches for funding of their liberation activities because they do not understand the connections between the economic workings of the capitalist system and racism.[7] Cone deems social analysis as imperative for liberation theology so that theologians know who the impoverished are, the reasons for their impoverishment, and who benefits from their poverty.[8] He consequently argues for the enmeshing of Christian faith and political praxis, explaining that "theology must actualize its Christian identity through social analysis and political participation on behalf of the victims of economic justice."[9]

Cone also notes the absence of any form of economic analysis in the practice of black theology. The black church and clergy have generally rebuffed radical economic analysis and Marxist social criticism because of the latter's alleged doctrine of "godless atheism." Cone submits that he and other early exponents of black theology ignored any reference to Marxist economic criticism because of the widespread fear of destabilizing America's conventional capitalist social and economic status quo.[10] Black theologians, he argues, must be aware of the dynamics of economic and social class in racist oppression; otherwise, their claims to represent oppressed black people become baseless.[11]

Cone concurs with the Marxian criticism that religion functions as an ideological mechanism of oppression. For example, the benign neglect of social analysis within black theology has contributed to the relative social conservatism of black clergy concerning women in church leadership and support of liberation struggles of other peoples of color.[12] Cone notes that the Christian churches of the United States have generally aligned themselves with capitalism, as

---

6. This point was made by James Cone in an interview with the author on Sept. 17, 1989.

7. Cone, *For My People*, 91.

8. Cone, *My Soul Looks Back*, 107.

9. James Cone, "Christian Faith and Political Praxis," *Encounter* 43 (Spring 1982): 139–40.

10. Cone, *My Soul Looks Back*, 94.

11. Ibid., 95.

12. Ibid., 16. Cone cites the speeches of Martin Luther King, Jr., to the Southern Christian Leadership Conference in Atlanta, Georgia, August 16, 1967, and states that David Garrow, a noted social biographer of King who wrote *Let the Trumpet Sound*, is convinced that King was a Marxist near the end of his life. This view,

opposed to standing with the victims of economic exploitation and oppression such as the poor, black men, and all women.[13] These churches have tended to equate the tenets of the Christian gospel with the values of monopolistic, individualistic capitalism, thus legitimating the white ruling class establishment. Cone urges the utility of the Marxist critique of capitalism within black theology to mediate the movement of liberation from capitalist mores.[14]

Culture and Gender in Black Theology

Cone views black culture as a source of black theology that is intimately connected to black experience and black history.[15] For him, culture must be defined in terms of the experiences of the oppressor and the oppressed. Jesus Christ related to the culture of the oppressed as he addressed the condition of the "concreteness of pain and suffering."[16] In a critique of Niebuhr's well-known typology in *Christ and Culture,* Cone portrays Christ as the liberator of culture for the culture of the oppressed, "taking the struggles of the little ones upon himself and transforming the actions for freedom into events of divine liberation."[17]

An awareness of the wellspring of African culture born on the African continent and its deep roots within communities representing the African diaspora worldwide is also reflected in Cone's writings. The history of Africans in Africa and the descendants of Africans in the Americas are inextricably intertwined, Cone contends, and this fact is important for the political struggles of all African people.[18] Black theology needs to use the vestiges and manifestations of Africanisms in black culture in America as a source for its practice, and in so doing American black theology will find a nexus with African theology on the African continent.[19] At the same time, there are distinctions between African and black the-

---

Cone says, is also held by the Democratic Socialists of America in a publication "From Reformer to Revolutionary." See *For My People,* chap. 4, n. 27.

13. Ibid., 182.
14. Ibid., 184 and 186.
15. Cone, *A Black Theology of Liberation,* 60.
16. Cone, *God of the Oppressed,* 90.
17. Cone, *A Black Theology of Liberation,* 90.
18. James Cone, "A Black American Perspective on the Future of African Theology" in *African Theology En Route,* ed. Kofi Appiah-Kubi and Sergio Torres (Maryknoll, N.Y.: Orbis Books, 1979), 179.
19. James Cone and Gayraud Wilmore, "Black Theology and African Theology" in *Black Theology: A Documentary History, 1966–1979,* ed. Gayraud Wilmore and James Cone (Maryknoll, N.Y.: Orbis Books, 1979), 469.

ologies, and therefore African theologies ought to be the prerogative of African theologians from Africa alone.[20]

Cone continues to be perturbed at the lack of sensitivity on the part of black male clergy concerning the practices of sexism and gender inequality within the black church. He faults black male theologians for their reticence on the question of male gender domination and their transmission of exclusively patriarchal traditions and sexist practices.[21] During the sixties and seventies these theologians dismissed the particularity of black women's experience under the rubric of other "urgent liberation goals" and the influence of a "white women's issue."[22] These male theologians simply laughed or insisted that black women were generally content with their subordinate gender positions in society. Black male clergy claimed that "black women really do like the role they play in the church."[23]

Male patriarchal attitudes held by black clergy are reflected in their persistent efforts to hold on to the reign of administrative power — efforts fueled by sexist dispositions.[24] Black women are virtually invisible in the ministerial leadership of black churches even though they constitute seventy-five percent of the black church community.[25] The seat of power in black churches remains in the hands of older male clergy. The National Conference of Black Churchmen, a radical black clergy coalition formed in the mid-sixties, refused to adopt a platform of equality for black women and would not change the word "churchmen" in its title to "Christians" until 1982![26] Cone is sharply critical of the posture of mainline black churches that are either indifferent to women's ministerial roles or adamantly opposed to women assuming leadership positions in the church. At the time of his writing there were no female bishops, college presidents, or general officers in the African Methodist Episcopal Church,[27] and this situation has changed only slightly since then. Cone contends that black male clergy need to pay tribute to the rigorous work of black women, whose tireless and unsung efforts have sustained the black church community for decades.[28]

---

20. Kofi-Appiah-Kubi and Sergio Torres, ed., *African Theology En Route*, 178.
21. Cone, *For My People*, 132.
22. Cone, "Black Theology and Black Women," 365.
23. Cone, *My Soul Looks Back*, 122.
24. Cone, *For My People*, 133.
25. Cone, "Black Theology and Black Women," 315.
26. Cone, *For My People*, 134.
27. Ibid., 133.
28. Cone, *My Soul Looks Back*, 22.

Desmond Tutu

Social Analysis and Black Theology

Desmond Tutu is a black liberation theologian in a very practical sense. Even though he has not written substantively on issues of social analysis in theology, he has demonstrated in his life and ministry of practice — through sermons and addresses, protests and marches — a model of theological resistance to the evil of racism in church and society.

Tutu is conscious of the evils of monopoly capitalism: he believes capitalism and the free enterprise system have victimized the black majority in South Africa.[29] Politically he identifies himself as a socialist, if pushed on that question,[30] and he criticizes industrial capitalism for its obsession with profit and its devaluation of the worth of the human person.[31] He argues that the western capitalist rhetoric of free enterprise is a myth that is used to exploit others and accumulate unregulated wealth.[32]

Tutu also takes the western European cultural precept of rugged individualism to task for its violation in South Africa of the African practice of communal ownership and corporate individuality — a practice that stresses organic interaction and collective responsibility.[33] Precisely for this reason Tutu rejects monopoly capitalism as the basis for the new society that South Africans are striving to build following the demise of apartheid.[34] Tutu recognizes that the internal dynamics of capitalism play themselves out in creating institutionalized hierarchical class structures which breed inequality. He notes that the apartheid regime in South Africa provides increments in social opportunities and economic benefits for a tiny sector of the colonized black majority, while forcing the bulk of the population to struggle under poverty-stricken conditions.[35] Tutu is well aware of the white ruling class rhetoric on urban black rights. This ruling class, of course is bent on retaining economic and political power and allowing a paltry sector of the black community to enjoy the privileges of good schools, high salaries, and social

---

29. Tutu notes this in the foreword to *Marx-Money-Christ*, ed. O. Hirmer (Gweru, Zimbabwe: Mambo Press, 1982).

30. Shirley Du Boulay, *Tutu: Voice of the Voiceless* (Grand Rapids: William B. Eerdmans Publishing Company, 1988), 236.

31. See Desmond Tutu, "The Bias of God," in *The Month: A Review of Christian Thought and World Affairs* (November 1989): 419.

32. Ibid.

33. Tutu, *Crying in the Wilderness*, 100.

34. Ibid.

35. Desmond Tutu, *Hope and Suffering* (Grand Rapids: William B. Eerdmans Publishing Company, 1983), 84.

mobility.[36] The distribution of wealth and resources among blacks and whites in South Africa, where seventy percent of the country's wealth is owned by the fifteen percent white minority community, is one of the results of this system of injustice.[37]

Culture and Gender in Black Theology

Tutu contends that Christianity in Africa must be wrapped in African garb and speak the language of African people. According to Tutu, the ancient near eastern world as described in the Hebrew Scriptures has much more in common with the experiences of African culture than western European culture.[38] Traditional religious concepts must be reclaimed and the richness of the African cultural past must be tapped in the evolution of black theology. The African notions of corporate individuality and the sacralization of the human person (*ubuntu* in Zulu and *botho* in Sotho), Tutu claims, can serve to inform paradigms of liberation from the fragmentation of blacks wrought by racism. He views black consciousness as imperative for the growth toward black liberation and holds the founder of the black consciousness movement in South Africa, Steve Biko, in high esteem. Tutu, in fact, identified Steve Biko's involvement in the liberation struggle, for which he was killed, as the epitome of Christian faith and practice.[39]

According to Tutu, black theology in South Africa also needs to address the question of the inequality of women under patriarchy, but he has not elaborated on the manner in which gender functions within the system of racist oppression and economic exploitation. He has not been as vocal on this issue as James Cone and has not raised it as a primary concern within his Anglican church community.

---

36. Ibid., 96. See also Tutu's article, "Tearing People Apart," *South African Outlook* (October 1980): 154.

37. Desmond Tutu, "Barmen and Apartheid" in *Journal of Theology in Southern Africa* 47 (June 1984). The grossly disproportionate disparity of wealth is further substantiated by the fact that four white corporations own eighty-one percent of the shares held in the Johannesburg Stock Exchange, Anglo-American Corporation alone controlling 60 percent of such shares. Cited in *South Africa Inc.: The Oppenheimer Empire* by David Pallister, Sarah Stewart and Ian Lepper (New Haven and London: Yale University Press, 1987), 37. As of 1993, Anglo-American controls 42.4 percent of the market capital, according to *The New York Times*, June 17, 1993. Further information on the vast wealth of these monopolies is found in Joseph Hanlon, *Beggar Your Neighbors: Apartheid Power in Southern Africa* (London: Catholic Institute for International Relations in collaboration with James Currey; Bloomington: Indiana University Press, 1986), 10.

38. Desmond Tutu, "Some African Insights and the Old Testament," *Journal of Theology in Southern Africa* 1 (December 1972).

39. Tutu, *Crying in the Wilderness*, 62.

Nevertheless, Tutu has made sporadic pronouncements on the subject of women's rights. He notes that patriarchal domination has been a stumbling block to women in society, as it was historically in the ancient near eastern world.[40] He also recognizes the necessity for an holistic concept of God that includes both genders created by the Creator.[41] The contradictions of gender equality and women's oppression derive from Eve's action in the book of Genesis, but a more accurate reading of Scripture reveals that women and men were meant to work alongside one another, not that men should rule over women. Tutu believes that, properly understood, the story of creation in Genesis 2 describes this complementariness.[42]

Tutu also understands that church teachings on the mutuality of women and men stands in contradiction to the practice of precluding women from the right to full ministerial authority.[43] While he understands the propensity for some women clergy to vie for positions shaped and defined by males in their efforts toward liberation, he recognizes the need for the right of self-determination and liberation of women as determined by women themselves. Ministerial models ought to be based on their creative potential as women, not merely on extending the essentially male hierarchical structure of ordained ministry.[44]

Tutu is well aware that the liberation of society as a whole is seriously incomplete without the integral liberation of women.[45] He believes that women have a distinctive contribution to make to the transformation of the world. Specifically, he maintains that women are those whose lives and experiences can restore the world's optimism and confidence in human nature since women tend to exhibit endurance and perseverance in the struggle for the realization of the optimal level of human potential. He bases this observation on the inherent qualities of God and the reproduction of these traits within feminine nature.[46]

In the context of apartheid society in South Africa, where they must endure the stigma of being both black and female, black women have exhibited exemplary courage in resisting the draconian laws of apartheid. Tutu lauds this level of resilience by black women whose Christian activism is witness to the dynamism of

---

40. Tutu, "Some African Insights and the Old Testament" in *Journal of Theology in Southern Africa* 1 (December 1972).

41. Tutu, *Crying in the Wilderness*, 120.

42. Tutu, *Hope and Suffering*, 150.

43. Tutu, *Crying in the Wilderness*, 119.

44. Ibid.

45. Naomi Tutu (Selector), *The Words of Desmond Tutu* (New York: Newmarket Press, 1989), 59.

46. Ibid., 61.

black womanist faith. In the impoverished community of Cross-roads, the huge slum outside Cape Town established by migrant women in their determination to live with their husbands who were forbidden under South African law to bring their families with them, Tutu saw a sign of hope that the struggle for liberation from racism and sexism would come to fruition with women leading the way.[47]

The vulnerability of children remains a special concern to the archbishop. He reminds his audiences again and again of the gross oversight and benign neglect that children suffer in adult dom-inated societies. His personal family experience has helped him realize the nature of this issue more profoundly.[48] In his advocacy of children's rights, he begins with the family unit expressing sensi-tivity to the fact that black liberation demands active participation of all sectors of society, especially the large component of youth and children.[49]

Similarities and Differences

Both James Cone and Desmond Tutu are Christian liberation theo-logians who perceive the Bible as the foundation of their theologies. Based on their respective interpretations of the biblical tradition, they conceive of God as God of the oppressed, standing with the oppressed classes of society. Cone is an academic theologian and has thus constructed a theoretical framework of social analysis in his theology, whereas Tutu is a practical theologian who acknowl-edges that his activism and clerical responsibilities have left him with little time to conceptualize the issue of social analysis in black theology in a more systematized manner.[50]

Secondly, Cone and Tutu would see black culture as a funda-mental source of their theologies, with Africa being an important point of reference for understanding black experience in both the United States and South Africa. Both theologians would view black culture in these places primarily as the experience of resistance to historical oppression. At the same time, black culture contains the ingredients for developing an alternative culture to that imposed

---

47. Ibid., 58. See also Desmond Tutu's article, "Persecution of Christians Under Apartheid" in *Martyrdom Today* ed. Johannes-Baptist Metz and Edward Schillebeeckx (Edinburgh: T. & T. Clark, Ltd., and New York: Seabury Press, 1983).
48. Tutu, *Crying in the Wilderness*, 121–22.
49. Ibid., 122.
50. This point was conveyed to the author in a letter from Archbishop Tutu, in 1990, in response to a questionnaire on social analysis methodology in theology.

by racist oppression, with Cone drawing upon African American culture and Tutu on culture on the African continent.

Thirdly, both Cone and Tutu are passionately committed to the church and to Christian ministry, although they recognize that there are oppressive practices found even in these institutions that they both respect and love. Cone appears to be far more critical of the role of the black church in the United States, especially on class and gender issues. Tutu is less critical of the church, probably because he is an archbishop within the Anglican church hierarchy and because black churches are generally more involved in the South African liberation struggle than their African American counterparts.

Finally, both theologians are critical of the practice of sexism in the church. Clearly, Cone is the more outspoken of the two, and criticizes the black church for its complicity in sexist behavior. Tutu, though expressing his abhorrence for sexism in the church, does not elevate the issue to the fore in his theology. The reason again may be his role as archbishop within the Anglican communion, a factor that compels him to moderate his criticism as the principal overseer within this church.

James Cone and Desmond Tutu have distinguished themselves as two insightful Christian theologians of our time. Their unflinching dedication to the liberation of oppressed peoples the world over, and particularly in the United States and South Africa, have made them leading protagonists of the liberation theology movement, particularly in the struggle against global racism. Desmond Tutu's courage, perseverance, resolve, and boldness, even in the face of seemingly insurmountable violent odds in South Africa, serve as an inspiration to oppressed peoples everywhere.

Cone and Tutu present constructive models for the use of social analysis in black theology. Both men are conscious of the roles of class, culture, and gender in this exploration. But do they adequately integrate these sociological dimensions into their fundamental theological reflections? This question will be considered in the following chapter as we reconstruct a model of a black theology of liberation by proposing an indigenous social analysis methodology.

Chapter 3

Radical Social Analysis Through the Black Folk Tale: Toward a Black Working Class and Underclass Theology of Liberation

Third World theologians have in the main moved from the luxury of just studying theology and theorizing about the peoples' struggle, from lines that follow as our academic or intellectual exercise, to the struggle of doing theology with the people. In their situation this is a life of struggle for a just society in this world.

—*Frank Chikane*[1]

Black theology will be relevant only if it speaks directly to the daily experiences of oppressed black people, particularly the black working class and the black underclass. In order to do so, it must evolve an indigenous methodology that is rooted in black culture and history. Yet how can black theologians *inform* the practice of black faith and concomitantly incorporate indigenous elements in the process of social analysis? One of the principal forms of doing black theology that has functioned historically to ensure the retention of the sacred ways of the ancestors and that is also instructive for social transformation is the black folk tale.

Stanley Hauerwas, a Canadian Christian ethicist, contends that "loss of narrative implies loss of community" and that "good and just societies require a narrative... which helps them to know the truth about existence and fight the constant temptation to self-

---

1. Frank Chikane, *No Life of My Own: An Autobiography* (Maryknoll, N.Y.: Orbis Books, 1988).

deception."[2] Social analysis in black theology is vital for freeing black people from self-deception and for stating the truth of black existence, with the objective of empowering black people to transform their existential reality. Theologians today are discovering that the folk tale and short story are coming to play an increasingly prominent role in the evolution of theological reflection as the means by which profound life truths and dynamic theological concepts are radiated.[3] This chapter will demonstrate that black theology can indeed utilize a narrative typology in the evolution of an indigenous social analysis methodology. Black theology cannot afford to neglect the contributions of African soothsayers who address the black experience through folk tales, art, and poetry, analyzing social, economic, and political structures in the process.[4]

Historically, folk tales have served to preserve the rudiments of people's cultures, especially the working classes and the underclasses who were constantly subject to the ideological control of ruling classes. The stories of the oppressed often functioned to remind the people of the ancient ways of their ancestors, making them conscious of their existential condition and of the value of their culture and humanity. In fact, folk tales affirmed the best of working class culture and tradition among many African, indigenous Indian, and Asian societies, working to unify fragmented communities into cohesive societies as each successive generation received renewed energy from recalling the resilience of the ancestors in times of distress.[5]

Folk tales and stories constitute a significant part of historical African tradition and culture, since African customs are often

---

2. Stanley Hauerwas, *A Community of Character: Toward a Christian Social Ethic* (Notre Dame: University of Notre Dame Press, 1981), 18.

3. Other theologians and ethicists that recognize the significance of the narrative tradition in theological discourse are Choan-Seng Song, *Tell Us Our Names* (Maryknoll, N.Y.: Orbis Books, 1986); James W. McClendon, Jr., *Biography as Theology: How Life Stories Can Remake Today's Theology* (Nashville: Abingdon, 1974); Robert Schooles and Robert Kellogg, *The Nature of Narrative* (London: Oxford University Press, 1966); Joseph Fletcher, *Situation Ethics* (Philadelphia: Westminster Press, 1966); George W. Stroup, *The Promise of Narrative Theology: Recovering the Gospel in the Church* (Atlanta: John Knox Press, 1981); Kim Chi-Ha, *The Gold-Crowned Jesus and Other Writings* (Maryknoll, N.Y.: Orbis Books, 1978); Michael Goldberg, *Theology and Narrative: A Critical Introduction* (Nashville: Abingdon Press, 1981); and Elsa Tamez, ed., *Through Her Eyes* (Maryknoll, N.Y.: Orbis Books, 1989).

4. G.-C. M. Mutiso, *Socio-political Thought in African Literature: Weisu?* (London: Macmillan, 1974), 3.

5. A good example of the dynamism of such tales is evident in the Japanese folk tale, "The Man Who Brought a Dream" and the Afghan tale "The Romance of Mongol Boy and Arab Boy," found among several others in Richard Dorson's *Folk-Tales Told from Around the World* (Chicago: University of Chicago Press, 1975).

transmitted via the medium of oral tradition.[6] Through the folk tale, aphorisms, myths, axioms, and proverbs were derived, serving to preserve the richness and fertility of the ingredients of African tradition. The African tale has long been a tenacious, indigenous cultural form which, notwithstanding the onslaught of European colonial imposition, has remained vibrant and outlasted the encounter with colonial European cultures.[7]

Further, folk tales and short stories are narrative forms that are instructive for describing social reality, for analyzing and interpreting the roles of the actors in such reality, and subsequently stimulating the imagination of the hearers and readers in transforming that reality. A classic illustration of the potency of short stories describing the socio-economic and political context of neo-colonialism in Kenya, for instance, is Ngugi wa Thiong'o's work *The Devil on the Cross*, which explicates the themes of neo-colonialist oppression, sexist subjugation of women, and the distortion of human social relations by monetary obsession as it has been evidenced in Kenya.[8]

The folk tale *Nomabhadi and the Mbulu Makhasana*, a narrative within the Xhosa-speaking tradition of South Africa, furnishes a vivid demonstration of the fertility of story within black religio-culture. *Nomabhadi and the Mbulu Makhasana* is a uniquely instructive story within the *ntsomi* genre in indigenous South African tradition that has served as a principal means of maintaining harmony and solidarity within historical South African society because it is a narrative that is "an affirmation of humanity in the face of constant threats of disharmony."[9] The *nstomi* tradition is distinctive in that it is primarily performed by women, with a "core-cliche"

---

6. Richard Dorson, ed., *African Folklore* (Garden City, N.Y.: Doubleday & Company, Inc., 1972).

7. Introduction to *Stories from Central and Southern Africa*, ed. Paul A. Scanlon (London: Heinemann, 1983), 1.

8. Ngugi wa Thiong'o, *The Devil on the Cross* (London: Heinemann, 1982). His other works, including *The River Between* (London: Heinemann, 1965), dwell on similar themes. Sipho Sepamla's *A Ride on the Worldwind* (London: Heinemann, in Association with Readers International, London and New York, 1984); *The Root is One* (London: Heinemann, 1979); and *Umhlaba Awethu* (Johannesburg: Skotaville Publishers, 1986) are also illuminating writings that have emerged from the struggle against apartheid repression in South Africa. In the United States, Toni Morrison provides an exemplary rendition of the power of black women's narrative in her work, *Beloved* (New York: New American Library, 1988), substantiating the view that black women's stories purvey the raw material for fertile theological conceptualization and practice. In Latin America, too, women theologians are also beginning to actively utilize the stories of indigenous Indian cultures in their theological deliberations. See for instance, Elsa Tamez, "Introduction: The Power of the Naked" in *Through Her Eyes*, ed. Elsa Tamez (Maryknoll, N.Y.: Orbis Books, 1989).

9. A. C. Jordan, trans., *Tales from Southern Africa* (Berkeley, Los Angeles: University of California Press, 1973), 154.

around which a narrative-plot is constructed.[10] Such traditions also reflect a purification quality in which the impurities of society are cleansed through the medium of conflict and transformed into stabilized social orders. The repetition of the core-cliche is instrumental in discerning the continuum between conflict situations and their resolutions.

Nomabhadi and the Mbulu Makhasana provides us with new vistas for black theological practice, especially in the task of social analysis and the accompanying emphases on the issues of class, culture, and gender. Our use of this tale represents an attempt to develop an indigenous social analysis method in black theology and suggests models that are instrumental in substantiating the theological deliberation toward black liberation proposed by black theologians such as James Cone and Desmond Tutu. In our analysis, portions of the tale will serve as ingredients for the elaboration of a narrative social analysis method that not only describes black suffering, but also implicitly contains the tools that could be used to transform such suffering. Special attention will be focused on the issues of class, culture, and gender as categories of oppression.

Nomabhadi Witnesses the Murder of her Brother

Nomabhadi and her family were forced to survive in desperately miserable and arid conditions precipitated by a severe drought that struck the rural community. Food that had been plentiful was now scarce, and hunger caused intra-familial tensions to rise. One day Nomabhadi's parents depart to work in the fields, and the three children, Nomabhadi and her two brothers, Ngubendala and Sihele, are left alone.

> One morning, after the parents had gone to the fields, Nomabhadi brought out some soup which her mother had left ready for the children to drink as soon as they got up. There was very, very little indeed, but as usual, Sihele had a little more than the others. As soon as the little bowls were put in front of them, Ngubendala looked at his share and looked at his younger brother's. Then he seized his bowl, drank the soup at one gulp, and then grabbed his younger brother's. Sihele held

---

10. For a more detailed explication of the *ntsomi* tradition, see Harold Scheub's introduction to *Tales from Southern Africa*, translated and retold by A. C. Jordan (Berkeley: University of California Press, 1973).

on, protesting aloud, and in the struggle all the soup spilled on the ground. In his rage, Ngubendala struck his younger brother on the head with the empty bowl and killed him.

Things had happened so quickly that Nomabhadi hadn't time to come between her brothers. When she saw what had happened, she buried her face in her hands and sobbed. Meanwhile, Ngubendala looked around in alarm, carried his brother's body to the edge of the enclosure, dug a shallow grave, and buried it.

He came back and sat sullenly next to his sister. Then, after a while he turned around and asked her, "Why are you crying, Nomabhadi?"

Silence.

Again, rather sharply, "Nomabhadi, why are you crying?"

"Because, because I — I'm hungry," she replied.

"Did you see anything?"

Silence.

"Nomabhadi, I'm asking you, did you see anything?" this time sharply and threateningly.

"N-no! I didn't see anything."

"All right, my sister. Stop crying now."

Ngubendala was sitting in a coiled up position, his arms rested on his knees crosswise, and his head rested on his arms. He was silent.

Nomabhadi slipped out of the courtyard quietly and walked toward the fields.[11]

In this account, certain metaphors symbolizing the dynamics of family interpersonal relations are implicit. This element of intra-familial ties is of vital import in systemic analysis, for the microcosm of individual experience in family settings plays itself out in the wider macrocosm of communal and societal experience. Conversely, systemic or structural social forces mould individual personality and behavior, underscoring the need for the integration of psycho-social and socio-economic analysis.[12] Such interaction is patent in the story of the death of Sihele at the hands of his brother Ngubendala.

---

11. Cited in *Tales from Southern Africa*, translated and retold by A. C. Jordan (Berkeley; Los Angeles: University of California Press, 1973), 157. For the complete version of the story, see Appendix A.

12. Archie Smith's *The Relational Self* (Nashville: Abingdon, 1982), for example, describes the interaction of psychic dimensions and systemic approaches in theological reflection.

The three children, Nomabhadi, Ngubendala, and Sihele, two males and one female, possessing unequal power in comparison with the adults, are left alone when their parents leave for the field. A power struggle erupts over food between the two male children. The stronger slays the weaker, and in a manner amazingly similar to the story of Cain's murder of his brother Abel in the book of Genesis, buries the body. The female child, Nomabhadi, cries at this unfurling of family tragedy and at her helplessness and inability to redress the situation. The older brother threateningly turns on his younger sister, compelling her denial of what she has witnessed. If she wants to live, then she must deny the evidence of her own experience. The elder brother lives in self-deception, at least temporarily. The sister escapes momentarily from the gruesome existential reality of family death. But the family will never be the same again.

Black Underclass Suffering

The excerpt of the Nomabhadi tale recounted here describing the murder of Sihele by his brother Ngubendala is metaphorical of the magnitude of oppression experienced by many black people in the United States and South Africa. Homicide is the leading cause of death of black men in the United States today. Young black men are forced by the conditions of economic deprivation, unemployment, under-education, and social alienation to eke out an existence within the confines of overcrowded concrete ghettoes by resorting to violent crime, drug peddling, and pimping. Human life has apparently lost its sacredness in those places where poor black life is viewed as dispensable. Self-respect among many black youth and respect for elders and women has reached an all-time low. Even the will to live itself has often been lost.

What are the causes of this crisis of underdevelopment and impoverishment of black life? Manning Marable, the noted political sociologist, contends that the socio-economic system of capitalism is essentially responsible for the condition of black suffering.[13] Between 1983 and 1989 there was an increase of wealth of the top one-half percent of the American population by $1.3 trillion and the correlational loss of $256 billion by the lower middle and

---

13. See Manning Marable's detailed and convincing analysis that confirms our convictions on this subject in *How Capitalism Underdeveloped Black America* (Boston: South End Press, 1983). E. Franklin Frazier's *Black Bourgeoisie: The Rise of the New Black Middle Class* (New York: The Free Press, 1957) is another excellent text for understanding the manner in which capitalism fostered poverty of the black majority while creating a tiny successful black middle class.

bottom classes over the same period, according to a study conducted by the Economic Policy Institute, a nonprofit think tank supported by labor and corporations.[14] These economic disparities result in poverty and racism, substantiating the claim that capitalism as a socio-economic system rewards the rich and penalizes the poor by helping the rich to grow richer and the poor to grow poorer. The superstructure of capitalism uses racism to produce an environment of material poverty and spiritual alienation, precipitating a mentality of callousness and desperate frustration among the poor, especially black youth.[15] Like Ngubendala murdering his brother Sihele, young black men and women confined to the underclass are compelled by existing circumstances and prevailing socio-economic and political structures to ventilate their sense of powerlessness and affliction by poverty on their kith and kin. The outlet for their innermost feelings of forlornness and despair, dejection and fatalism becomes their sisters and brothers around them, as they externalize their internal aggressiveness against the system. They are unable to get at the capitalist edifice that pulverizes them of their beings and devalues their lives by refusing to provide them with decent education, proper shelter, adequate health care, and fulfilling employment. Their animosity against the system is catapulted back into their souls and bodies as they seek the means to exorcise themselves of the anger besieging their beings by unleashing it on fellow black people.[16]

In South Africa, the ruling regime of F. W. De Klerk has recently talked much about the "new South Africa" and argued that apartheid is past history. Yet the objective conditions that black people experience indicate little respite from poverty, hunger, illiteracy, homelessness, and continued exploitation as cheap labor. Though apartheid has been officially repealed, white domination and black suffering is more pronounced than ever before. For instance, some seven million black people still do not have decent housing. Hun-

---

14. *Post Tribune,* Gary, Indiana, October 30, 1992.

15. One of the best texts that delineates the effects of capitalism on the so-called black underclass with accompanying statistics, is Manning Marable's *How Capitalism Underdeveloped Black America* (Boston: South End Press, 1983). Another informative work is Douglas Glasgow, *The Black Underclass: Poverty, Unemployment and the Entrapment of Ghetto Youth* (San Francisco: Jossey Bass Press, 1980).

16. See William H. Grier and Price M. Cobbs, *Black Rage* (New York: Basic Books, 1968) for a psycho-social reflection of the frustrations of black people in their attempts to confront racism and oppression in America. For an elucidation of the psychological dimensions of the struggles of black people facing the pathology of racism in South Africa, see N. C. Manganyi, *Being-Black in the World* (Johannesburg: Study Project On Christianity in an Apartheid Society and Ravan Press, 1975) especially ch. 6, "Reflections of a Black Clinician."

dreds of thousands of black children still do not attend schools for lack of facilities. Poverty rates for people living in many rural areas is close to seventy percent. It is evident that the rhetoric of the white ruling class in South Africa claiming that black people have no basis to continue the liberation struggle since South Africa is now a free country does not sound convincing to the black majority who are still colonized in the land of their birth. It must be noted that the current agenda for change is continually determined by the apartheid regime. The African National Congress, the leading organization currently negotiating with the regime, has progressively compromised on key issues to the point that its original program of liberation has largely been abandoned in favor of power sharing with the minority regime.[17]

The conditions facing black people in the townships of South Africa, like Soweto, Alexandra, Kwa Mashu, Crossroads, and New Brighton, are not fundamentally different from those of black people living in the American ghettoes of Harlem and Bedford Stuyvesant in New York, Watts in Los Angeles, and Roxbury in Boston, though they may differ in scale and scope on occasion. Poverty, widescale unemployment, violent crime, overcrowded living conditions, and lack of proper recreational amenities prevail in these areas. It is no wonder that Soweto has one of the highest crime rates per capita in the world. Many black people continue to be victims of homicide and fratricide, while members of the privileged ruling elite pride themselves on living the "good life."

Sihele's slaying by his brother Ngubendala is metaphorical of the atrocities committed against black people by the capitalist system, forcing them to live in overcrowded ghettoes where seething frustration eventuates in internecine conflict and homicide. Black men are often killed by the bullets of nervous or trigger-happy police or shot by fellow black people involved in the drug trade or in syndicated crime. A fifty-percent unemployment rate for black youth makes this segment of the population an ideal target for recruitment by sophisticated crime networks. How else would the poor survive in a system in which it is necessary to have money to live and often the only way to earn this money is through crime? The high crime rate results in more law enforcement officers who are responsible for policing poor neighborhoods and who end up arresting hundreds of thousands of black men. The judicial system then sends such per-

---

17. See the *Chicago Sun Times* article, "Deal Would Put Off South Africa Democracy," February 8, 1993. Though leaders within the ANC, such as president Nelson Mandela, vehemently deny that the ANC has agreed to a power-sharing arrangement with the apartheid regime, it is clear that such a "deal" has been made, as the article reports.

sons to prison for long terms or executes them, depending on the nature of the crime and the state in which it was committed. South Africa and the United States are credited with the dubious distinction of having the highest execution rate per capita in the world. This vicious cycle is indicative of the institutionalized violence of the judicial system that incarcerates black people because they are poor and defenseless. If the judicial system does not destroy them, homicide and fratricide does.

Today, the United States has more people in prison than any other country, including China with its population of 1.2 billion people. There are over one million people serving prison terms, of which fifty percent are black! The number of people in U.S. prisons doubled in the 1980s, with sixty-three thousand new prisoners added in 1989 alone. There are now more black people between the ages of twenty and twenty-nine entrapped within the penal system than there are in college.[18] Such facts call the claim of the United States as the leader of the "free world" into serious question.

In South Africa, one of the most crucial issues facing the black community in the struggle for liberation from apartheid capitalism is the issue of state-sponsored violence in black townships under the guise of liberation. Black people are regularly gunned down by killers hired by the regime to destabilize the black community.[19] One state-sponsored group, the Inkatha Freedom Party led by Gatsha Buthelezi, who is a paid appointee of the white government, continues to collaborate with apartheid structures in the name of freedom. Thousands of black people in Natal province have been affected by the violence of Buthelezi's Inkatha party, and this situation has been seized upon by the western media as a classic instance of "black on black violence" and has been used to the political capital of the apartheid regime. The subtle innuendo from such biased coverage is that black people are unfit to rule themselves, let alone anyone else, in South Africa. The derivative sentiment is

---

18. Cited in *World Press Review*, November 1992, 41.

19. These waves of killings continue unabated. See for instance, *The Post Tribune*, Gary, Indiana, April 20, 1993. The newspaper article reported that nineteen black people were killed in drive-by shootings in the black township of Sebokeng and in Vosloorus. From the vantage point of black people, the regime is ultimately responsible, even though government surrogate organizations are often the actual perpetrators of violence. The question that black people raise is: If the regime was so effective during the sixties and seventies in hunting down black activists fighting apartheid through its massive security apparatus, why is it that the white state is currently either unable to find the culprits responsible for assassinating black people or powerless to control its military forces in situations of peaceful protest? These events lead many black people to believe that the regime is the principal protagonist in the violence against black people while mouthing the rhetoric of peace, reconciliation, and freedom.

that apartheid may not be as repugnant as it seems, since it is still administered by "civilized" white people. Though concrete evidence such as the South African Police-Inkathagate funding scandal has corroborated the fact that the regime has been engaged in an intense program of subversion of black political organizations through systematic assassinations of activists and blaming such violence on "factional" violence, the western media has generally ignored such contrary points of view.[20]

It may very well be that, as Nomabhadi later became the source of hope and courage within that context of suffering, black working class women will also contribute significantly toward preventing internecine conflict between organizations. Nelson Mandela echoed this hope at his first political rally shortly after his release from prison, in Durban, South Africa, on February 24, 1990.[21] Just as Nomabhadi's troubles were caused ultimately by the poverty and hunger experienced by the people of the village, the root cause of all the current violence in South Africa lies in the structural violence of apartheid that violates the essential humanity and dignity of all black people and dehumanizes white people.

A word needs to be said about the "underclass," since the term is used throughout this chapter. This sector of the black community constitutes a subclass even below the ranks of official workers. People in the underclass are more often than not unemployed, underemployed, homeless, illiterate, day laborers, farm workers, children, and those who have been uprooted from their ancestral lands and left to die in poverty-stricken and barren rural reserves. Many are women and children. Members of this class generally live with no housing or residential rights, often in shack dwellings with

---

20. News of the "Inkathagate scandal," as the press described it, broke in late July 1991. *The Weekly Mail*, a prominent weekly newspaper, openly published the secret memoranda describing the South African police funding of Inkatha. The South African police helped establish a black surrogate union called United Workers Union of South Africa (UWUSA) which was affiliated with the Inkatha Freedom Party led by Gatsha Buthelezi and continued to fund the union to the tune of one and a half million South African rand ($500,000). The objective of this project was to foment discord over the issue of sanctions, since UWUSA was committed to staving off the call for economic sanctions against the South African regime, while the majority of black people in the country supported sanctions. The point of the eruption of violence in Natal must be situated in the context of funding of UWUSA. Violence peaked in December 1989 when 212 people were killed and March 1990 when 353 people were killed. Was it totally coincidental that this escalation of violence occurred around the same period that the state funded two Inkatha rallies in Natal? Liberation organizations believed that it was not. The regime had provoked the violence by supporting the anti-sanctions rallies in the black community, realizing that many were already opposed to the lifting of economic sanctions. See detailed documentation published in *The Weekly Mail*, July 26–August 1, 1991.

21. *New York Times*, February 25, 1990.

no electricity, sewage, running water, or basic welfare provisions. In South Africa there are an estimated six to seven million people who fall prey to apartheid's policies and have been fined, arrested, and jailed for living in areas declared illegal for black occupancy in white South Africa.[22] These persons have had their dilapidated and scantily furnished homes demolished by bulldozers clearing areas for white industrial development — areas like Crossroads, a community of close to four hundred thousand people on the outskirts of Cape Town, and Emzomusha, outside the east coast city of Durban, with over five thousand people.[23]

The underclass represents the most marginalized and exploited sector of South African society. It consists of people who have absolutely no protection under apartheid's laws; they are simply viewed as "illegals" in the eyes of the governing authorities. The apartheid system treats them with maximum disdain and wishes them obliterated, sometimes literally crushing them into the dirt and dust. This policy of social annihilation takes its toll on black families, especially in the rural Bantustans where it breeds a despondency which leads to disease and death.[24]

The predicament of the black underclass is vividly captured in the description of Sihele's murder by his brother, Ngubendala. It is a sobering reminder of the gravity of pain and the excruciating agony that poor black people experience in the inner cities of America or the Bantustans and townships of South Africa. Women, the elderly, youth, and children especially find themselves trapped within the cages of violence fostered by a socio-economic system that denies people their fundamental humanity solely on the grounds of race. The overwhelming masses of black people who live in South Africa's Bantustan reserves experience the kind of poverty, social isolation, and unemployment that Nomabhadi and her family underwent. They are often forced to sojourn long distances to the urban areas to seek work in the capitalist-owned mines and factories. As we noted earlier, the Bantustans function as a reservoir of cheap labor for the development and expansion of white industrialization. Those black persons who fall outside the quota necessary for production

22. *Sunday Tribune*, Durban, August 7, 1989.
23. The author was able to observe first-hand the deleterious effects of these demolitions in Cape Town and Durban in the summer of 1988. The story was also described in the front page article, "Thousands Homeless in Natal Shack Fires" in *City Press* newspaper, Johannesburg, August 28, 1988.
24. See for example, *Relocations: The Churches Report on Forced Removals*, published by the South African Council of Churches and the Southern African Catholic Bishops' Conference, 1984, 32. See also M. Nash, *Black Uprooting from White South Africa: The Fourth and Final Stage of Apartheid* (Johannesburg: South African Council of Churches, 1980).

in the mines and factories are left to die from the poverty and harsh climatic and agricultural conditions in the reserves, while South Africa exports an abundance of foodstuffs to Europe, North America, and Japan.

The Black Church's Response to Oppression

As much as the account of the fratricide of Sihele by his brother, Ngubendala, symbolizes the atrocities perpetrated by the violence of racist and capitalist structures, it also recalls the Christian community to the consciousness of human sinfulness. Regardless of their socio-economic and temporal location in history, human beings are often prone to selfish actions. There is a penchant for evil action within the constitution of human nature, and the sin that oppressed people commit is that many collaborate with their oppression as a means to survive. Many revolutionary movements of liberation in history have gone astray when leaders claiming to champion the cause of freedom of the oppressed have sought to perpetuate themselves in positions of power.[25]

It is precisely in this area that Martin Luther's teaching on the redemption of humanity by God's grace strikes a responsive chord. Regardless of what humans accomplish or engage in, they are still subject to the limitations of being human. They are inevitably finite creatures in God's sight and thus can never hope to justify themselves or make themselves deserving of God's love and grace, for they have acted selfishly and destructively at one time or another.[26] All fall short of God's glory, as the apostle Paul declares in his letter to the Romans. Therefore, no human being can become deified and no human institution can become absolutized. Though human beings are created in God's image, they are still capable of sinful actions that deny the imprint of God's image within their beings. Luther's perception of the saving grace of God is a

---

25. For a socio-political analysis of the failure of revolutionary movements in the "Third World" in recent history, see Gerard Cheliand's *Revolution in the Third World* (New York: Penguin, 1975). For an ethical critique of the potential of revolutions to become distorted, see Gerard Fourez, *Liberation Ethics* (Philadelphia: Temple University Press, 1982).

26. This insight is expressed by Simon Maimela in "Justification by Faith and its Continuing Relevance for South Africa" in *Theology and the Black Experience*, ed. Albert Pero and Ambrose Moyo (Minneapolis: Augsburg Press, 1988), 39. This anthology of writings by black Lutheran theologians from the United States and South Africa represents the diverse views and reflections of black people in the struggle for liberation in the practice of the Christian faith from a Lutheran perspective.

constant reminder of the abiding love of God in the face of human sinfulness.[27]

Even while participating in movements of socio-economic and political transformation, the task of the black theologian is still to recall the course of struggle to remain beholden to the gospel of Jesus Christ. Though demanded by the Christian faith, deep involvement in the black liberation struggle is not synonymous with the totality of God's reign because of the finitude of human potentiality. The murder of Sihele by his brother Ngubendala makes humankind recognize the limitations of human nature, a theological motif that black working class and underclass theologies of liberation cannot afford to overlook. In response to situations of deprivation as depicted in the Nomabhadi story, black churches are called to be prophetic as a consequence of the realization that their ultimate allegiance is to God. They are challenged to uphold the central tenets of the Christian gospel: unconditional love, justice, equality, and interdependent community. They must resist those structures that produce situations of suffering and violence as described in the story of Nomabhadi's family, whose poverty and hunger led to Sihele's murder by Ngubendala. They cannot afford to simply treat the symptoms and effects of the policies of oppression; they must attack the root causes of these conditions and participate in movements of protest for the positive abolition of such injustice. The churches cannot be silent in the face of the expanding black underclass trapped in the miasma of poverty, unemployment, disease, and despair. They must engage in concerted efforts of conscientization, that process of education which seeks to empower oppressed people to become conscious of their oppression by socio-economic structures and to transform their lives from conditions of deprivation and indignity to one of life in abundance, as Jesus proclaimed in John 10:10.[28] These proposed actions imply a politicized church community that is in the forefront of socio-political struggle. Such a role represents a continuation of the original mission of the black church in the United States and the indigenous African

---

27. Jaroslav Pelikan and Helmut T. Lehmann, *Luther's Works*, Vol. 26 (St. Louis: Concordia, 1955), 361.

28. The term "conscientization" was originally coined by the noted Brazilian educator Paulo Freire. His philosophy and methodology of education is illuminated in such works as *Pedagogy of the Oppressed* (New York: Continuum, 1968); *The Politics of Education: Culture Power and Liberation* (South Hadley, Mass.: Bergin & Garvey Publishers, 1985); *Cultural Action for Freedom* (Boston: Harvard Educational Review and the Center for the Study of Development and Social Change, 1970), and with Antonio Faundez, *Learning to Question: A Pedagogy of Liberation* (Geneva: WCC Publications, 1989).

churches in South Africa: religious communities immersed in the movement against enslavement and for justice.

Doing black working class and underclass theology involves standing unwaveringly on the side of persons in these classes. Such persons are the most victimized by racism and hence possess the greatest potential toward overthrowing the yoke of oppression because they have little vested in the perpetuation of the current status quo. They have everything to gain from its demise and its supplantation with a socialist alternative.[29] In this connection, black churches can no longer radiate an ambiguous political and economic disposition. They need to realize that they cannot totally embrace the interests of the black middle class that benefits from the United States' and South Africa's current social and economic arrangements and in the same breath profess to be communities of liberation.

The vagaries of capitalist evolution in the United States since the beginning of the Reagan era have escalated unemployment within the life of the black community, affecting poor youth in particular. Mammoth U.S. corporations have sought places abroad in Africa, Asia, and Latin America where local elitist governments have institutionalized cheap labor policies to create favorable climates for the injection of western capital and the agglomeration of corporate profits. This efflux of capital and closing of local production plants has severely damaged the domestic economy, causing hardships for the large working class in the U.S. The lack of employment, educational opportunities, and economic incentives has consequently forced many black youth to turn to crime and the underground economy of drug dealing. This underground economy is estimated to be worth over $200 billion today, a subsector that the American capitalist economy has bred, nurtured, and thrives upon to a significant extent.

The black churches must re-arm themselves with a radical black working class and underclass theology of liberation. Many of them must discard their generally collaborationist and accommodationist theologies, so that they can become tangible instruments of liberation. They ought to formulate programs that are directed toward equipping unemployed black people with educational skills and technical expertise as a solution to the immediacy of oppression, uneducation, unemployment, and deprivation. The period of

---

29. This point about the prerogative of oppressed peoples is made by Gustavo Gutierrez, the Latin American liberation theologian, echoing educator Paulo Freire's views on the subject, in *A Theology of Liberation* (Maryknoll, N.Y.: Orbis Books, 1971), 235.

preoccupation of many black churches with bake sales, expansion of church buildings, and furnishing of the interior is long gone. If black churches intend to be relevant to concrete black social experience, they must propose and implement programs that are designed to uplift and mobilize working class and underclass people.

The black church as the historical home of the impoverished needs to continue to be the place of refuge for such persons every day of the week, not just on Sundays. More churches need to conduct programs that feed the hungry, while simultaneously challenging those socio-economic structures that breed poverty. Poverty is neither a desirous nor a romanticized condition; on the contrary, poverty is scandalous and unacceptable in this day and age. In challenging the sources of poverty, the black church would be retrieving the prophetic character that distinguished its historical formation.

The Christian education, youth, liturgical, homiletical, and outreach programs of black churches must be refurbished and fundamentally reoriented to respond to the deep-seated frustration, anger, and inertia on the part of many in the black underclass and working class. This ministry must engage in the psychic liberation of persons in these classes, so that they can be transformed into bold and invigorated individuals freed from captivity to racist and capitalist ideologies. Freeing the mind is a prerequisite for individuals who wish to free themselves from the oppressive structures of society. Steve Biko, the founder of the Black Consciousness Movement in South Africa, contended that "the most potent weapon in the hands of the oppressor is the mind of the oppressed."[30] Black churches can do much to influence the minds of black people through sermons, musical selections, symposiums, and other educational components of church ministry, especially in reinforcing the point that the political and economic liberation of black people is not only consistent with the Christian gospel, but is the demand of the gospel in the black community. In the United States, black churches could also work to enlighten black people on the significance of Africa and the vibrance of African working class culture in the overall struggle for national liberation.

---

30. Steve Biko, *I Write What I Like* (San Francisco: Harper & Row, 1978), 92.

Nomabhadi Encounters the Deceptive Mbulu

Because of the famine in their village, Nomabhadi's parents' requested that Nomabhadi go to her uncle's village, where food was in plenty. They admonished her never to cry or to look back or to the left or the right; if she did, she might encounter the dreaded Mbulu. Nomabhadi sadly left the village, as her parents requested. Yet unable to resist one final look at her parents, she turned around, only to see that her parents had burnt themselves to death in their hut, for there was no more food in the village.

As she turned to resume her journey, she remembered her mother's warning that she was not to cry, and she quickly checked her sobs. But her first cry of pain had been heard, for she heard a strange voice calling to her in a lisp, "Sister! Sister! Why are you crying? Wait for me."

With a start, Nomabhadi wiped away her tears and, before she knew what she was doing, she had looked left and right to see where the voice was coming from. A strange creature had just emerged from the thicket and was running to overtake her. It was half-human, half-beast. It was walking on its hindlimbs but could not hold its body up. Its body was wrapped in the skin of some animal resembling the baboon, but much bigger. What she could see of its face was human, but all the facial bones were sticking out and the cheeks were hollow, as if they had been sucked in. Its body was hard and dry, as if drained of all blood and water. Its hands were coarse and bony, and its nails long and ugly. It had a long, lively tail that contrasted with the tail of the baboon-like animal whose skin this creature was wearing.

"Don't be afraid of me," it said as it overtook her. "I am your sister. Stop crying and tell me your name."

Nomabhadi had heard descriptions of the Mbulu many times, and the appearance of this creature, its manner of speech, and its voice tallied so well with these descriptions that she knew at once that this was one. But this Mbulu was kind and called her "sister." So why should she fear it?

"My name is Nomabhadi," she replied, trying to smile.

"Nomabhadi, Nomabhadi," the Mbulu said repeatedly. "It's a nice name, a very nice name indeed."

"And what's *your* name?" asked Nomabhadi.

"Oh, just call me 'sister.' I'll tell you what. Let's just call each other 'sister.' I'll call you 'sister' too, though I like the name Nomabhadi very much. Nomabhadi, Nomabhadi." The Mbulu repeated the name over and over again as they went along, but all the time with the lisp that Nomabhadi had already noted.

Interestingly, the event of the Mbulu deceptively courting Nomabhadi somewhat resembles the account of the temptation of Adam and Eve by the serpent in the Garden of Eden narrated in Genesis 3. The surrender to temptation by the evil one is also a recurring theme in the Nomabhadi story. In the above passage satirically describing Nomabhadi's encounter with the dreaded, lisping, but "beautifully ugly" Mbulu, certain motifs can be discerned that are instructive for the use of a social analysis methodology in black theology.

The Cultural Temptations of Capitalism and Elitism

The Mbulu tempted and successfully wooed Nomabhadi through its crisp voice and attractive personality, similar to the manner that capitalist society tempts the working masses. Capitalism projects an extravagant aura, maintaining a profile of glitter that is enhanced by the most advanced technological sophistry and genius. It often promises long-term prosperity and assurance of unbridled material possessions.[31] It exhibits the finest delicacies in food and clothing, thereby promoting a culture of elitist privilege and excessive indulgence. It engenders an insatiable appetite among middle class people for consumer goods and modernized gadgetry that stimulates the desire for an opulent lifestyle. Such materialist aspirations are generally depicted as the ultimate ideal of human civilization in capitalist society.

As a socio-economic system, capitalism has been obdurately committed to the accumulation of profits by the white ruling classes in the United States and South Africa. One of the means by which it has successfully accomplished this monopolization of wealth and riches for the minority capitalist class is its rhetoric of market economics and consumerism. It has created privileged elitist communities in the process, but does not tell people that it is necessary to possess much money to survive at a basic level and be happy in a capitalist system. It has been able to disseminate the myths of democracy and individual freedom through extensive networks of mass communication and the marshaling of capital resources.

---

31. See Erich Fromm, "The Sane Society" in *The Capitalist System: A Radical Analysis of American Society*, ed. Richard C. Edwards, Michael Reich, and Thomas E. Weisskopf (Englewood Cliffs, N.J.: Prentice-Hall Inc., 1972), 267, for an in-depth description and analysis of the socio-economic excesses of capitalist culture.

Capitalist culture enshrines the doctrine of rugged individualism and institutionalizes competitiveness, thus cultivating humanity's basest instincts.[32] It valorizes money, making monetary accumulation respectable while diminishing the sacredness of being human. Concealed beneath the veneer of prosperity and extravaganza lies a gruesome reality of squalor and deprivation for the masses of black people and other peoples of color. On the surface, capitalism strives assiduously to convey the impression of liberality and beauty. But internally it reveals a vulturous and parasitic nature, where gluttonous money-mongers thrive on emaciated and impoverished children, women, and men who are forced to slave to satisfy the fastidious economic and social diet of the capitalist. No other economic system impoverishes over 2.5 billion people today, almost half of the world's population and many of them people of color. Why is it that while "currently, sufficient land, energy and water exist to feed well over twice the world's population," hundreds of millions still go hungry?[33] Black theology must become unafraid of naming the principal obstacle to the attainment of black liberation: capitalism.

Black working class and underclass people are wage slaves under the global system of capitalism, constantly tempted by the trappings of a deceptive and corrupt system. The capitalist system speaks in a seductive voice via commercials and hollow rhetoric, as did the Mbulu in calling out to Nomabhadi, reminding us vividly of the voice of the serpent in the Garden in the book of Genesis. All too often, black people who have experienced oppression and deprivation for generations through slavery or apartheid find themselves tempted by the indulgences of capitalist culture. Capitalist culture degrades workers, objectifies women, belittles children, alienates the elderly, canonizes individualism, and nourishes racism for the purpose of monopolizing economic power. The ornamentation of the good things of life is consistently held up before the petit-bourgeois sector of the oppressed black community to siphon them into the spiral of such culture. These tactics are pursued with the objective of legitimating and normalizing an essentially unjust and exploitative system.[34] Radical black working class and underclass culture, symbolized by Nomabhadi's resilience, can function as a vehicle

---

32. Frederick J. Perella, *Poverty in American Democracy: A Study of Social Power* (Washington, D.C.: Campaign for Human Development, United States Catholic Conference, 1974), 72.

33. Quoted by the Earth Save Foundation and cited in *The Washington Spectator*, a biweekly publication of the Public Concern Foundation, 19. 2 (January 15, 1993).

34. Richard Edwards, Michael Reich, and Thomas Weisskopf, eds., *The Capitalist System*, 267–68.

to stop the movement of capitalist culture diffusing itself into the contours of black society.

Nomabhadi's Parents Appear to Her from the Earth

Nomabhadi had been virulently deceived by the subtle Mbulu and ended up as a "dog" at the house of her relatives, as the Mbulu cunningly adorned her clothes and threatened to kill her if she told the truth to her aunt and uncle. She regretted her weakness and disregard of her parents' warning never to look back. She had lost her piece of bread, her clothes, and her name to the Mbulu, and now she was being treated as a dog in her family's household!

> It was too much! She just wanted to die.
> She seized the scaring-stick and struck the ground hard with it, calling out aloud: "Open, O Earth, and swallow me, for I've no mother and no father!" Thereupon the ground began to shake where she had struck it, then it opened and behold! There were the shades of her parents standing in an open grave.[35] They had brought her plenty of food, clothes, and beautiful ornaments, and without saying a word, they held these up to their daughter. She received them with great joy, first the food, which she laid aside on the green grass, and then the clothes and ornaments, which she put on immediately. Then she settled down to eat while the shades of her parents watched silently.
> As soon as she had finished eating, the shades held up their arms, indicating that everything was to be handed back to them. Nomabhadi took off the clothes and ornaments, packed them and handed them back to the shades together with the mats and bowls and cups in which the food had been served to her. Then the shades vanished and the grave closed and everything was as it had been before.
> This made Nomabhadi very happy. She no longer wished to die, for now she knew that her parents wanted her to live.

Nomabhadi's despondency at her situation of being humiliated while at her relatives' home, subject to the treatment of a dog while the Mbulu played her role of niece, knew no bounds. She just wanted to die, as her parents had.

---

35. "Shades" refer to the ancestral spirits in African religio-culture.

Despair is Transformed into Hope

The predicament of Nomabhadi is akin to the millions of black people in the United States and South Africa. The conditions of dispossession, homelessness, unemployment, illiteracy, and hunger precipitated by capitalist exploitation provokes deep despair among them. Such experiences "induce hopelessness and damage people's self-esteem both personally and as a family," making them "feel threatened and unable to cope with their bewildering predicament."[36] They are similar to those of Nomabhadi, who was reduced to a subhuman existence characterized by total despondency. The feeling of rejection and powerlessness felt by black working class and underclass people in the United States and South Africa is overwhelming, to the point that people often wonder, "Where is God?" The task of the theologian and of the religious community is to respond to this question and to proclaim the hope of the gospel of liberation from a predicament of dire oppression.

Nomabhadi's parents miraculously appeared to her from the earth and infused her with the spirit of life. The inculcation of hope in the hearts of the oppressed is a principal imperative in the life of the black church in the liberation struggle against oppression and exploitation. Hope is an essential prerequisite for the mobilization of women and men in the resistance movement, to empower them to overcome the element of fear provoked by the awesomeness of these oppressive systems. Even at the nadir of their suffering, black people ought never to allow the evil one to subdue their resolve to eliminate apartheid and capitalism; rather, just as with the eventual fate of the Mbulu, they ought to be determined to bury these evils forever.

The spirit of the Creator known so powerfully in Jesus and the ancestors of Africa nourishes black people's determination to overthrow their oppressors. The Holy Spirit is perceived as the power that instills courage and determination in the hearts and minds of working class and impoverished black people. It represents the movement of oppressed people and ignites the flame of refusal to cooperate with repression and economic exploitation. It inflames the hearts and wills of black working class and underclass people, so that they unflinchingly declare: "Better to die on our feet than to live on our knees!"[37] The power of the Holy Spirit of Yahweh dem-

---

36. The South African Council of Churches, *Relocations: The Church's Report of Forced Removals,* published by the South African Council of Churches and the Southern African Catholic Bishops' Conference, 1984, 31.

37. This was the slogan of the white abolitionist John Brown during the campaign for the eradication of slavery in the United States.

onstrated so poignantly in the crucifixion and resurrection of Jesus informs such perseverance. The Holy Spirit is thus a revolutionary force that urges the black oppressed to rebel and overthrow the evil of oppression, using all of the marshaled forces at their disposal. It is the catalyst that brands the notion of selflessness and fearlessness into the constitution of black being so that black working class and underclass people are able to resist the seductive tentacles of capitalism and challenge the system at its roots. It dispels every taint of anxiety and uncertainty, uplifting the oppressed when they have fallen and raising them to new heights when they are sunk or temporarily submerged in the mire of despair. The Holy Spirit is God's way of ensuring that God's reign and transformation of all creation becomes a living reality in this world.

Oppressed people have a responsibility to be true to their Creator who created human beings in God's image with the inviolable right of being free creatures. Any power that obstructs this assertion of freedom is diabolical and, like the Mbulu, inimical to the Spirit of God. When Nomabhadi agreed to walk with the Mbulu against her parents' wishes, she capitulated to the power of evil, as oppressed people often cooperate with the evils of capitalism and elitism.

Working class and underclass black theology announces hope that is grounded in daily acts of resistance to the tyranny of apartheid, capitalism, and neo-colonialism.[38] Such proclamation of hope necessitates practical involvement on manifold fronts so as to make God-experience become a living and meaningful reality. In the South African context, it implies radical theological praxis that is expressed in the following measures:

1. Rejecting all apartheid structures, including the currently orchestrated "democratic" elections under the auspices of the white minority regime.[39]

2. Struggling for the return and restoration of all land from which black people have been historically dispossessed by European

38. Neo-colonialism refers to the condition of economic dependence of many formerly colonized countries in Africa, Asia, and Latin America on the previous "mother" countries of Europe and North America, even though these former colonies claim independence. Further, these independent countries are subject to the political and economic control of the industrial colonial powers.

39. See David Mermelstein, ed., *The Anti-Apartheid Reader* (New York: Grove Press, 1987), especially ch. IV, "Racial Capitalism," for an illumination of past black boycotts of white-controlled elections like the tricameral parliamentary elections held in 1983, resulting in the launching of the United Democratic Front. The refusal of many black people in Soweto to pay rent to the municipal authorities is one instance of the refusal to cooperate with apartheid structures delineated in "Soweto's Three Year Boycott" in *Work in Progress* 59 (June/July 1989).

colonialism and initiating self-help programs for education, nutrition, and community empowerment, especially among communities like Crossroads outside Cape Town, Duncan Village outside East London, and Emzomusha on the outskirts of Durban.[40]

3. Intensifying the resistance of black workers in unions and other worker collectives for justice and protection of worker's rights, such as the National Union of Miners and the Black Union of Miners. The black church must continue to play a positive role in enlisting material and financial support for workers dismissed for striking or arrested by police.[41]

4. Serving as the voice of the voiceless wherever black communities do not have a voice because of repressive structures.

5. Enlisting support for the national liberation movements especially at this stage of the liberation struggle: the Azanian Peoples' Organization (AZAPO) and the Pan Africanist Congress of Azania.[42]

6. Strengthening the movement of the total divestiture of foreign capital from South Africa currently and calling for mandatory and comprehensive economic sanctions against South Africa,

---

40. A good example of an organization that is engaged in black working class and underclass empowerment in Natal province, for instance, is the Natal Advice Center Association, a nonracist group that functions to assist black people in gaining information about access to facilities for health care, employment, worker support, and counseling. Again, though not always politically radical, it nevertheless addresses pressing black concerns on the level of urgency and immediacy. See *NACA: One Year On,* a booklet published by the Natal Advice Center Association, 1989. Other advice associations affiliated or associated with the Azanian People's Organization, such as Kopanong Community Center in Dobsonville, Soweto, are involved in some of the most important grass-root organizing activity within the black communities of South Africa. Suffice it to say, the situation of black poverty and oppression has not fundamentally changed since the official abolition of apartheid statutes in 1991. The bulk of South Africa's land area still remains in white hands.

41. The South African Council of Churches has been especially supportive of detainees and workers arrested by police through its Dependants Conference.

42. The ANC is not included here because as an organization it has opted to collaborate with the apartheid regime and agreed to jointly rule South Africa with the regime for the next five years. It has thus ceased to be a liberation movement in the sense that it is no longer engaged in the struggle to be totally free from the apartheid regime but rather views itself as a political party within the current landscape of apartheid politics. It has also abandoned its original anti-capitalist and pro-socialist platform. See, for instance, the article "Deal Would Put Off S. Africa Democracy" in *Chicago Sun Times,* February 4, 1993. The spirit of reconciliation that de Klerk displays does not include the release of all black political prisoners who have used force to destroy apartheid. There are still members of the Azanian Peoples' Organization who are being held in apartheid jails, according to the president of the organization in 1991, Pandelani Nefolovhodwe.

until the white ruling class is sufficiently weakened economically to the point that it will be ready to surrender real political and economic power to the black majority.[43]

7. Raising the consciousness of South African society on the evils of sexism and engaging in concrete programs that redress the inequality of black women aggravated under apartheid and capitalism, through organizations such as Imbeleko, the United Women's Congress, Natal Federation of Women, the Federation of South African Women (FEDSAW), and the Transvaal Federation of Women.

8. Working tirelessly in the overall struggle for the construction of a nonracist, democratic, indivisible, and socialistic nation, predicated on the principles of indigenous culture that accord respect to Mother Earth, and where racism, capitalist exploitation, environmental despoliation, and sexism are positively abolished.

Such actions indicate the political nature of doing radical black working class and underclass theology in South Africa. Doing theology is thus a "dangerous business"[44] in a context like South Africa, especially in the task of building a socialist society. Socialism is proposed because it promises participatory democracy, where all people, especially the working class, actively participate in the political and economic processes on an egalitarian basis. It institutionalizes social and economic equality where the land, resources, and fruits of industrial production are communally owned by the people and shared equally among them. Under the envisaged socialist system, no individual or organization would be permitted the right to become wealthy through profit accumulation, while many are impoverished. Rather, income levels for all vocations, regardless of status, would be egalitarian, so as to ensure justice and fairness for all citizens. Most importantly, the provision of adequate housing, decent health care, free education from elementary

---

43. This is an important call, especially in the wake of the recent conflict between the South African state and the ANC over the issues of a one person, one vote democracy and an interim government. The ruling regime in South Africa is clearly prolonging the negotiation of the nation's freedom as long as possible, so that the entire process will become too exhausting and eventually will be scuttled. Divestment and sanctions thus need to be enforced until such time that liberation of the South Africa nation is "irreversible" and the apartheid regime is overpowered to the point that it has no choice but to discuss *genuine* democratization of the country.

44. An expression used by Allan Boesak, the South African theologian and cited by Bonganjalo Goba, in "Doing Theology in South Africa: A Black Christian Perspective" in *Journal of Theology in South Africa*, 31 (June 1980).

through university levels, and gainful employment would be considered fundamental human rights assured by the political order and economic dispensation. The distinctiveness of this form of indigenous socialism is that it subscribes to a model of national economic development that accords sacred respect to Mother Earth and creation.

In the United States, radical black theology must function in empowering poor and working class black people to challenge the edifice of oppression through massive education and mobilization programs that are oriented toward self-determination. Such organizing can be mediated through the formation of alternative community bodies that are geared toward decent education, proper health care, and job training, while concomitantly politicizing the black poor on the need to overcome oppressive structures. Black churches must become the sites of black people's empowerment where the gospel of hope can take on new meaning for a people besieged by the spirit of hopelessness similar to Nomabhadi's sense of dejection. The inner feeling of hopelessness felt by the black underclass must be exorcised by the effusion of the spirit of Jesus that rebels against every oppression, as the parents of Nomabhadi infused her with hope toward transformation.

The understanding of Jesus Christ, who is at the heart of the Christian revelation, is key within this context of black liberation theology. The experience of Jesus Christ is not confined to an abstract figure who lived about two thousand years ago in Palestine; Jesus is also perceived as an oppressed and exploited working class and underclass person who is most vividly encountered in the struggle to overcome the crucible of racist and capitalist oppression. Jesus is black and identifies with the working class and underclass, especially with women and young people. He is pro-liberation and anti-exploitation.

The Power of the Ancestors is Reflected in Mother Earth

The act of Nomabhadi's parents reaching out to her from the earth is metaphorical of the power of Mother Earth itself. In African tradition and many other indigenous cultures, the ancestral spirits are said to reside in the earth. This perception is observed, for instance, in the practice of the pouring of libations on the earth prior to an African feast.[45] Respect for the ancestors of black people in

---

45. John Mbiti renders a detailed explanation of the veneration of the departed and the rituals and practices associated with the passing of loved ones, such

the United States and in South Africa today is equally important in the black liberation struggle, for was it not the struggle of the African ancestors to preserve their own historical traditions that made it possible for black people to walk on Mother Earth today? Black people in the United States must reclaim their African heritage more vigorously and incorporate historical African cultural practices into their contemporary lives. This is the only way in which they can overcome the alienation fostered by the dominant American culture and confront the legacy of slavery that stripped them of their historical African languages, customs, and identity.

Nomabhadi felt abandoned to the point that she considered suicide. Yet was this her parents' wish in sending her away? On the contrary, right at the juncture that she was close to surrendering her life, her parents appeared to her in the earth below. She was ecstatic. She realized that she was not alone. Her parents were watching over her and rescued her from possible death. One of the cardinal tenets of the African tradition is the sense of continuity with parents, grandparents, and their descendants, a belief that God's Spirit is revealed in the spirit of the ancestors.[46] In fact, the ancestors are believed to be mediators between the Creator and humanity. They are always revered because they are believed to preserve the harmony and stability of community.[47]

The earth, as the repository of the spirits of the ancestors, functions in the story as the residential home of Nomabhadi's parents. The earth is seen as a living being within the train of African religio-cultural tradition, and if the foundational theological view of black churches in the United States is to become working class at its roots and Africanist in its outlook, the churches will need to undergo a cultural transformation. Africanist working class theology takes the preservation and sacralization of the earth as a primordial theological principle. It laments the fact that the earth has been despoiled and brutally exploited for commercial gain, disregarding her sacred role as a living being, the Mother Goddess. In concert with retrieving their African roots, black churches need to become involved in the wider political and economic struggle against the environmental

as parents and grandparents, in *An Introduction to African Religions* (London: Heinemann, 1975). See especially chapter 11, "Death and the Hereafter," 110–25.

46. In the Zulu language of South Africa, "Nkulunkulu" is the word that refers to God. It also translates as God being the great ancestor of humanity. See E. W. Smith, *African Ideas of God* (London: Heinemann, 1950), 102–12.

47. See for example, Harry Sawyer, *God: Ancestor or Creator?* (London: Longman, 1979) for a treatment of the theme of the significance of ancestors and ancestral spirits within the framework of African religio-culture.

abuses of capitalism that pollute the air and Mother Earth's rivers and streams.[48]

The consequences of adherence to this indigenous African principle are serious. Black churches would be moved to confront United States oil corporations such as Exxon, Chevron, and Shell, that continue to dump hazardous waste products into the ocean and contaminate underground drinking water systems, often located close to low income black and brown communities.[49] Black Christian churches would thus enter into coalitions with other communities such as the American Indians, the Black Muslims, and the environmentalist movement to resist "environmental racism."[50]

In the cosmologies of indigenous peoples of color around the world, the earth ultimately belongs to the Creator. To perceive the earth in monetary terms and to utilize it for profit is to insult the Spirit of the Creator. To put land up for sale as a piece of real estate is to desecrate Mother Earth. As part of the ongoing black liberation struggle, black churches must become part of the move to preserve Mother Earth and conserve her precious resources so that life on this planet can be preserved for future generations.[51] In this manner, the black churches would do justice to the generations of African ancestors buried on American land. African blood flows with that of the indigenous Indians of this continent through the experience of slavery. The Indians historically

---

48. For a concise essay on the policies and practices of the U.S. government on this issue, see chapter 2, "The Politics of Pollution" of Joseph M. Petulla's *Environmental Protection in the United States* (San Francisco: San Francisco Study Center, 1987).

49. A typical instance of this abuse and disrespect for the earth was evidenced in the oil spill and environmental contamination by Chevron Oil Company in Richmond, California, in October 1988. Chevron's oil refinery is located adjacent to a low income black community. The toxicity of waste substances released by this energy corporation has resulted in disease and impaired the longevity of health of many of these local residents.

50. The term "environmental racism" was popularized by Benjamin Chavis, formerly chairperson of the Commission on Racial Justice in the United Church of Christ and now executive director of the National Association for the Advancement of Colored People (NAACP), in an attempt to explain the policies of corporate America that established toxic waste and dumping sites often close to impoverished black communities.

51. A sector of the Euro-American community, among them churches and theologians, have attempted to trace the trajectory within Euro-American and European Christian traditions that revere creation. They have become involved in environmental and ecological preservation movements and with community groups like the Rainforest Action Network in the United States. For an illumination of the creation tradition within Euro-American Christianity, see *Cry of the Environment*, ed. Philip Joranson and Ken Butigan (Santa Fe, N.M.: Bear & Co., 1984). See also the poster, "I am Anishinabe" by Dennis Banks, published by the American Indian Movement in San Francisco in 1982, that calls people to listen to the ways of Mother Earth.

provided refuge to African slaves running away from white slave-masters. Through solidarity with Indian people, black people would be according recognition of the indigenous Indians as the sole legitimate custodians of this land who were dispossessed by European colonialism.[52]

Black churches and Indian land rights organizations, such as the International Indian Treaty Council based in San Francisco, California, need to work together on issues of self-determination and protection of Mother Earth. It is through such collaboration that black people could initiate a dialogue with their Indian blood-relatives on the question of living on native lands, particularly in light of the systematic dispossession of black people.[53] Black people in the United States would thus retrieve elements of their African cultural heritage by living more closely with the indigenous Indian nations, since Indian and African peoples share much in their cosmology concerning respect for the earth and communal ownership.

The conjunctive liberation movement of the black churches and Indian people signifies a fundamental rejection of the dominant Euro-American cultural norms that reward community competitiveness and valorize profit-making over communal sharing. It implies a qualitatively different cosmology that is neither steeped in the crass materialism of European industrialism nor anchored in the idealism of the era of romanticism.[54] As Nomabhadi was nourished by the spirit of her deceased parents, the spirit of oppressed

---

52. This very important historical linkage has been generally ignored by most historians and black organizations. More works on this subject have appeared recently, an informative piece being William Loren Katz's *Black Indians: A Hidden Heritage* (New York: Atheneum, 1986).

53. Black people who have lived on small farms in the Deep South in states like Mississippi, Alabama, Georgia, and Texas for several decades have had their land base seriously eroded since the beginning of this century. Since that time, black farmers in places like Lexington County, Mississippi, have lost huge tracts of lands to white industrialists and wealthy farmers since they did not possess the capital and machinery to cultivate these lands. As a consequence, many poor black farmers have been forced into a condition of sharecropping or working as farm hands on white farms. The author has had first-hand experience of this process of land dispossession of poor black farmers in Tchula, Mississippi in December 1988 during a tour of that state. The Rural Organizing Crisis Committee in Tchula is one organization working to protect the livelihood and preservation of the land base of the remaining black farming population. Over 110 million acres have shifted from black farmers to wealthy white farmers since 1910. Lee McGee and Robert Boone's work, *The Black Rural Landowner: Endangered Species: Social, Political and Economic Implications* (Westport, Conn.: Greenwood Press, 1979), provides further details on this subject.

54. American Indian Movement leader Russell Means furnishes a critique of western European enlightenment thought in "The Same Old Song" in *Marxism and Native Americans,* ed. Ward Churchill (Boston: South End Press, 1983), 28.

black and Indian peoples will be renewed by the adherence to the wisdom of the ancestors.

Nomabhadi Destroys the Mbulu with the Help of the Village Folk

Upon discovering who the Mbulu really was and that Nomabhadi had been cheated by the evil creature, the community folk resolved to find a way to trap the heinous Mbulu. They set a trap for him by asking all persons who had spent the night in a hut with three elderly women of the village to jump over a pit the next morning. (This was part of the pre-marriage custom that the Mbulu had to fulfill since it was playing the role of Nomabhadi, who was of marriageable age). They would then discover the source of the evil that had made eerie noises in the hut the night before. When it came to the Mbulu's turn to jump, he attempted to hide his protruding tail. Alas! His hidden tail flew loose and he fell into the deeply dug pit. Immediately, some men filled the pit with earth and buried the Mbulu alive. That night Nomabhadi slept soundly. She rested in preparation for her marriage rites. On the evening of the first day of seclusion, Nomabhadi was lying peacefully when she suddenly heard a "thud-thud" coming toward the hut. She listened carefully and wondered who it was. She heard a faint voice calling,

> "Ntonjane (young girl), who are you with in there?"
> "I'm alone," she replied.
> Thereupon a huge melon came leaping into the hut.
> "I'm going to kill you!" shouted the melon.
> "You'll never kill me!" shouted Nomabhadi, leaping to her
> feet.

It was the Mbulu, in the form of a melon! The melon flung itself at her twice. She caught it and threw it hard on the ground, trying to crush it. Nothing happened to the melon. It quickly made for the door. The women outside the hut heard the commotion and came running. Nomabhadi explained that the Mbulu had returned. Swiftly, the head of the house took an ax and went straight to the Mbulu's grave, from which a wild melon plant had grown. That plant had given rise to the Mbulu in the form of a melon, and the man vigorously chopped at the roots until the plant was finally uprooted at its foundations. He burnt the area where the melon tree had grown and everything was reduced to ashes. Nomabhadi was finally freed from the evil Mbulu. She emerged from the hut, looking more beautiful than ever before.

Oppressed People Must Be United
in Order to Overcome Oppression

One of the relevant motifs that can be discerned from this final sequence of the Mbulu's defeat by Nomabhadi and her uncle's community folk is the instrument of familial solidarity and community interdependence in the staving off of evil. Nomabhadi was unable to destroy the demonic Mbulu on her own accord. The entire community was involved in the battle. The destruction of the Mbulu by the community members acting in concert with one another demonstrates the collective role of liberation practice. Such unity and organic action is imperative in the struggle against oppression.

Black churches must strive for unity among black political groups, especially where there are tactical differences between organizations that have radical responses to black oppression.[55] The Bethlehem Lutheran Church in Oakland, California is just one illustration of the type of unity among such groups that can be mediated by black churches. A strong philosophy of Pan-African socialism is espoused at Bethlehem Lutheran Church, and the faith affirmation of the community is prophetic Christian radicalism. This church community serves as a beacon of hope and a symbol of resistance for African and other oppressed working class people, and the political disposition of this religious community has attracted native American activists and liberation leaders from Southern Africa, the Caribbean, Palestine, and Asia. Likewise, the story of Nomabhadi teaches black people and other oppressed people an illuminating lesson: factionalism sows the seeds of disunity within the ranks of the liberation movement, while organic resistance serves to unify powerless and oppressed people. Unity is vital particularly in light of the fact that no singular black organization alone can liberate black people.

The Holy Spirit intends that the oppressed working class and underclass black people struggle together as children of the one God. It moves to unite oppressed peoples. Such unity accords well with some of the foundational principles of the Christian gospel: communal interdependence and collective sharing, reflected in the

---

55. Rev. Canaan Banana, the former president of Zimbabwe, makes this point in *The Gospel According to the Ghetto* (Harare, Zimbabwe: Mambo Press, 1981), 50.

teachings of Jesus and evidenced in the early Christian community.[56]

Communal solidarity and organic individuality are pivotal in occluding the imposition of singular and isolated cultural forms of individuality wrought by western European industrialization and capitalism. Such insular values are inimical to the collectivist sense in Christian teaching.[57] Developing this level of critical and collective consciousness is a precondition for the intensification of the struggle for liberation against oppression.

The Power of African Women in Effecting
Creative Transformation

Finally, the story of Nomabhadi and the Mbulu Makhasana reminds us of the resilience of women in the struggle against the evil of oppression. Doing black theology demands addressing the oppression of women on the grounds of race, sex, and class. The irruption of female humanity is a striking theological sign of the times. Black women have demonstrated historically that they will not tolerate social and political oppression as suggested by the massive demonstrations against passbook laws in South Africa in 1958. Yet women are accorded secondary status when it comes to decision-making, within both religious institutions and the ranks of the liberation movement.[58] The potency of black women's thought and activity offers new paradigms of liberation activity that are qualitatively different from that of men because of women's distinctive historical experience and culture. Such a model serves to enhance the entire black liberation project.[59]

The peculiarity of women's experience of oppression under colonialism and capitalism and their creative responses in challenging these systems must be tapped as a source for the engagement of liberation theology among black people. It is high time for the voices of women to be amplified, both in current theological circles and the broader society. The liberation of black society must include the emancipation of all sectors of the society from sexist practices and conditioning.[60]

---

56. Insightful work on this subject has been done by Canaan Banana, in *The Gospel According to the Ghetto* (Harare: Mambo Press, 1981), 49.

57. Buti Thlagale, "Towards a Black Theology of Labor," a paper from a 1983 seminar on Black Theology entitled "Revisiting Black Theology," 29.

58. Sibongile Makhabela's article "Women and Liberation" in *UMTAPO Focus,* August 1988: 7, published by UMTAPO Center, Durban, South Africa, provides an incisive treatment of this theme concerning women's oppression and liberation.

59. Ibid., 8.

60. Dabi Nkululeko's article, "The Right to Self-Determination in Research: Aza-

Bell Hooks, a black scholar, has written much in this area that can be instructive for theologians. She contends that a redefinition and expansion of the understanding of feminism is needed, one that expands on the confluence of the factors of race, sex, and class within the configuration of women's struggle.[61] She balks at the divisive tendency by some activist groups in the U.S. that insist on labelling persons as either feminist or anti-racist. She proposes an organic, systemic-analytical approach in the feminist movement, confirming our principal argument that socio-economic analysis is imperative for understanding the causes of oppression in order to suggest appropriate liberating theological responses to such oppression.

Hooks' critique is insightful for the understanding of the organicism of the factors of race, sex, class, and culture that constitute the phenomenon of oppression. She assists white feminist theologians in expanding the epistemological horizons that inform their criticism, so that these theologians can incorporate such factors into their theologies. Hooks also aids black male liberation theologians in integrating the issues of race, sex, class, and culture in the effort toward black liberation. Her perceptions substantiate the proposition of a black working class and underclass theology of liberation.

The feminist notion that is conceived in this context is not a mere supplantation of patriarchal structures. Neither is it oriented toward an inclusion within already distorted and domineering patriarchal forms. On the contrary, it suggests an entirely new manner of interpreting religious tradition, Scripture, and all other social reality based on the experiences of poor black women. Mercy Oduyoye, a West African theologian, asserts that such a feminist consciousness in theology ought not to be the province of female theologians alone, but that all persons doing theology ought to reflect this holistic perspective. She maintains that such womanist reflections are vital to all black and African theologies.[62]

In the light of this critique by women theologians, black churches

nia and Azanian Women," in *Women in Southern Africa,* ed. Christine N. Qunta (London, New York: Allison & Busby Limited in Association with Skotaville Publishers, Johannesburg, 1987), 104, is resourceful for an understanding of the pain that black women particularly have had to endure in order to be heard.

61. Bell Hooks, *Feminist Theory: From Margin To Center* (Boston: South End Press, 1984), 25. Hooks also explicates the interplay of the factors of race, class, and sex in the oppression of poor black women in *Race, Sex and Class* (Boston: South End Press, 1984), and more recently in *Black Looks: Race and Representation* (Boston: South End Press, 1992).

62. Mercy Oduyoye, *Hearing and Knowing* (Maryknoll, N.Y.: Orbis Books, 1986), 121.

are called to work actively to redress the gender imbalances foisted by patriarchal society on the black church and to embrace the creativity of womanist theologies. In the story of Nomabhadi's defeat of the Mbulu, the men possessed immense physical strength in covering the grave and uprooting the melon tree, yet needed the spiritual resolve of a woman like Nomabhadi to obliterate the evil Mbulu. Such an event is a reminder of God's creative wisdom that accorded women and men power and status that are equal though different in composition.

Complementary division of labor serves to undermine oppressive structures that favor one gender group over another. Women and men are integral to the being and existence of each other. Though men have been conditioned to dominate women because of their masculine physical power, they need to realize that women are human beings who "hold up the sky" and possess strength in ways that no man can match. The best illustration of the ability of women to endure untold pain is a daily experience that is often taken for granted: the agony of childbirth. According to physiologists, childbirth is a process that men are physically incapable of bearing, and ironically without which no man would have been brought into existence. It is the femininity of women that furnishes the ingredients for some of the most imaginative theological expressions known in human history. The perseverance of African women during the slavery epoch in America, for instance, produced much of the underpinnings of the theology of resistance to the practice of slavery and was subsequently diffused into the prophetic tradition of the black church.[63]

Doing black working class and underclass theology involves appropriating the stories of the mothers and sisters of the black community whose experiences are so fertile with theological richness and creativity.[64] Black churches can no longer afford to push the concerns and distinctive contributions of poor black women to the periphery. God's voice speaks most resoundingly from the pain

63. Alice Walker's work, *You Can't Keep a Good Woman Down* (New York: Harcourt, Brace and Jovanovich, 1981), 119, elaborates this theme of struggle even in the face of being overwhelmed by the odds.

64. In this regard one need only cite such works as Toni Morrison's Pulitzer winning work, *Beloved* (New York: New American Library, 1988); *Sula* (New York: Knopf, 1974); *Song of Solomon* (New York: Knopf, 1977); and *The Bluest Eye* (New York: Holt, Rinehart and Winston, 1970) and Alice Walker's *The Color Purple* (New York: Harcourt, Brace and Jovanovich, 1982) and *Meridian* (New York: Harcourt, Brace and Jovanovich, 1976) as possible sources that depict the struggles of poor black women against sexism, racism, and classism. Such narratives serve as excellent material for the development of a social analytical methodology in black liberation theologies.

and struggles of this bottom-most sector of the oppressed community. The struggles of poor black women can serve as an important point of departure in black theology's deliberation toward liberation.

Black churches cannot proceed with business as usual by conforming to a mainstream society and culture that generally deprives black women from realizing their God-endowed potential as human beings. Black women, particularly working class and underclass women, need to be actively incorporated into all levels of decision-making in the life of the church. Considering that close to three-quarters of the active members of black churches are women, such a demand is far from unreasonable. Black male clergy must desist from tenaciously holding on to their ecclesial positions in the name of being "God's servant" while the sisters are widely denied basic rights and privileges. The presence of black women in church pulpits and functioning as ministers ought to become as normal as attending church every Sunday. Such practice is part of the black cultural transformation of which the black churches must become active participants.

This process of consciousness-raising must involve more black male clergy and pave the way for the recruitment of more black women into the corridors of theological education so as to prepare them for leadership roles within the life of black churches. Black male theologians and clergy must reflect more positive attitudes toward black women generally and working class and underclass black women in particular.[65]

It is only through this radicalizing of black theological practice that the black church can indeed become a community of empowerment, where God's presence is most poignantly reflected and the incarnation of Jesus' spirit is most dynamically witnessed.[66] The myth, for instance, that black women in the United States are better off than their male counterparts due to affirmative action programs in education and employment needs to be challenged through educational forums of the church. Black women, youth, men, and children need to comprehend the historical social role that African women have played in liberation struggles notwithstanding the severity of being raped, socially abused, and economically trampled on by structures of slavery and oppression.

---

65. For a treatment of this theme of the need for restructuring of attitudes toward women, see the article by Georgina Jaffee and Collette Caine, "The Incorporation of African Women into the Industrial Workforce: Its Implications for the Women's Question in South Africa" in *After Apartheid*, ed. John Suckling and Landeg White (Center for African Studies: University of London in Association with James Currey and Africa World Press, Trenton, N.J., 1988).

66. Jon Sobrino, *The True Church and the Poor* (Maryknoll, N.Y.: 1984), 197.

As part of their educational and consciousness raising programs, black churches need to work earnestly toward reversing some of the hostilities that have emerged between many black women and black men because of dominant cultural norms like rugged individualism and sexism. A cultural transformation within the life of the black churches can begin to end the gender tensions and rivalries fostered by a fundamentally oppressive society.

Black working class and underclass men need to realize that engaging in liberation practice also implies reflecting a liberated attitude toward their sisters. The axiom of gender complementariness and of harmonious coexistence of sisters and brothers derived from the foundational African tenet of relationality can be best exemplified within the life of the black church. This practice would serve as confirmation of the Christian teaching that women and men were created by God for mutual communion with each other.

Conclusion

The model of black theology and social analysis based on the folk tale suggested in this chapter encourages black working class and underclass people in the United States and South Africa in their endeavors toward socialistic liberation and self-determination. The obduracy of monopoly capitalism necessitates a rededication of black working class and underclass women and men to the intensification of the struggle for liberation and creative transformation. It must not weaken black people to the point that an aura of resignation sets in where people acquiesce and retort: "If you can't beat them, then join them." Black working class and underclass theology is at variance with such a resigned position and takes issue with tacit acceptance of any form of injustice — racism, capitalism, colonialism, classism, sexism, or any other exploitative system or order. It is directed toward participatory democracy on a socialistic and communalistic basis in which there is a socialization of the land and all production so that black people can actively determine their own destiny.

The elevation of the issues of class, culture, and gender in this model of black theology confirms the contention that radical social, economic, and historical analysis is indispensable to the project of black theology. Black theology will be relevant to the black experience of oppression only if theologians are also skillful and rigorous social and economic analysts. There is no easy route for the path of the black theologian within the contours of liberating theological discourse: the edifice of capitalist civilization as a globally oppressive and exploitative system must be analyzed and critiqued at its very foundations, revealing the interfacing of the dynamics of race, class, culture, and sex in the causes of oppression.

Black theology must continue to function as a weapon at the discursive level. Most importantly, it must become a tangible instrument that could be utilized for the material liberation of all black people from the yoke of capitalism, apartheid, and colonialism. It is through working class and underclass culture that this liberation theology can become a spear in the armor of black working class and underclass warriors. Within this configuration, the voices of working class black women may well be the echo of God that reverberates through the corridors of the ghettoes, townships, barrios, and reservations of the United States and South Africa. These voices need to be heeded so that the creative energies of poor women previously denied within theological exploration can be best incorporated into new paradigms of doing theology.

Black working class and underclass religio-culture must serve as a primary point of departure in the practice of black theology. It is through the lenses of these classes of women and men that the Bible comes to assume new meaning and is transformed into a narrative of liberation. Indigenous black working class culture possesses the ingredients for engaging in radical socio-economic and historical analysis, as the tale of Nomabhadi and the Mbulu-Makhasana demonstrated. All black theologians of liberation would be remiss in their task of reflection on God's Word in the world if they neglected the stories of working class and underclass black people, especially those of women. Perhaps this mode of black theology will be the vehicle through which African peoples will be able to contribute effectively toward giving the world what it so desperately needs: a more humane face. This book is geared toward propelling all persons committed to the liberation of the oppressed and oppressors everywhere and the transformation of all creation in that direction.

Epilogue

It has been some twenty-five years since James Cone first published his pointed theological work, *Black Theology and Black Power.* Much has changed since the penning of that text, and much has remained intact in terms of the tenacity of racial domination and economic exploitation. Capitalist power appears more solidified than ever before, especially with the recent downfall of eastern European socialism. The capitalist powers of the world, notably Japan, the United States, and West Germany have now consolidated the capitalist enterprise, reinforced by the rhetoric of the western media that now heaps praises on the achievements and wonders of monopoly capitalism. Democracy is thus equated with western monopoly capitalism and the laissez faire system.

The arduous research undertaken in this book shatters the fallacious assertion of the laurels of the capitalistic system. Capitalism continues to be a pernicious socio-economic system, particularly exploiting impoverished people of color and marginalizing all working class people. It is a resilient and tenacious system that has come back fighting and is continually able to adapt and modify itself in the most unpredictable forms. Yet such a pertinacious character by no means implies the moral correctness of this foundationally exploitative and inherent evil order; rather it suggests that capitalism is a powerful institution that is so influential precisely because it has at its disposal the vast resources of the world that it has expropriated for the past five centuries. Its obsession with power and profit knows no bounds.

The Holy Spirit of God, who has been active among the lives of African people for generations, continues to be a dynamic force in the struggles of the oppressed black working class and underclass peoples of the United States and South Africa, impelling them to radical action. Just as Nomabhadi was successful in destroying the evil Mbulu and Jesus broke the fetters of the tomb on Easter morning, the black working class and underclass peoples in the United States and South Africa will also experience a day of resurrection.

The United States will be exorcised of its colonialist and capitalist character and transformed into a truly democratic and free nation. In this new society, the first people of North America, the indigenous Indians, will live as sovereign nations and have their confiscated lands returned to them. There can never be lasting peace in the United States so long as justice is denied to the indigenous people. Society must pay homage at the outset to the initial rights of the indigenous people of this land, since their ancestors still reside in the earth of North America. To disregard this primordial consideration would be to violate the spirits of the ancestors of the native peoples. Liberation and transformation of the United States behooves the precondition of the implementation of the fundamental right of the indigenous Indians to national and territorial sovereignty.

The new United States, or Turtle Island, as this continent was called by the Indians prior to the advent of Europeans, will be a society in which race, culture, class, and gender no longer operate as categories of oppression but rather function as incidental adjectival descriptions. People will be recognized as sacred creatures created in God's image. The black working class and underclass in the United States, in conjunction and concert with other oppressed peoples, such as the indigenous Indians, and the working class Latino, Asian, and Euro-American communities, will strive to build a new socialistic and humanistic society that is characterized by participatory democracy in the political, economic, social, and cultural spheres. No longer will a tiny Euro-American elite be permitted to wield a monopoly of wealth so that the top one percent of American society controls over half of the country's wealth, as under the present capitalist socio-economic arrangements. Instead, the wealth produced by the working class will be shared and redistributed equitably among the working people of the United States.[1] The radical involvement of black working class and underclass peoples in the United States would by no means tarnish the commitment of black peoples to their motherland, Africa. It would merely imply a broadening of this transformative vision, so that all godless oppressors and God-fearing oppressed peoples are totally liberated.

The post-capitalist and post-apartheid societies in the United States and South Africa will also need to embody an ethic that institutionalizes the respectability for all of creation, particularly

---

1. Manning Marable renders one vision of the specifics of this liberated society in his article "The Third Reconstruction: Black Nationalism and Race Relations After the Revolution" in *Socialist Visions,* ed. Steve R. Chalom (Boston: South End Press, 1983).

Mother Earth. The earth is a living being whose creative potential and reproductive capacity gives life and who is thus venerated
within African and indigenous Indian religio-culture. Mother Earth
has been desecrated by the tide of western European industrial civilization and now needs to be left to follow her own natural course
of evolution. Materialistic culture has already wrought irreparable
damage to the ecosphere, the land, and the water systems of the
earth.

Black working class and underclass theology, as the story of Nomabhadi so graphically illustrated, displays a profound reverence
for the earth. Doing black liberation theology would entail the rejection of the exploitation of creation and the commodification of the
earth. In the post-capitalist, decolonized American society, the land
will be restored to its sacral character and not viewed as a piece of
real estate to be developed or as a source for profit agglomeration.
The destruction of rainforest areas like that of the Puna rainforest
in Hawaii,[2] the redwood forests of the northwest, and natural areas
like Yellowstone, as well as the contamination of the air by toxic
gases released from industrial plants, would have to be terminated
in this new society.[3]

In the new South Africa, the colonial era will be abolished to pave
the way for a liberated Azania, where all people will live in a new society that is just and harmonious.[4] The principle of nonracism will
be the social principle on which the post-apartheid society will be
constructed, where race will no longer be a determinant of people's
humanity. The land will be redistributed with justice among the
landless black working class and underclass who have been historically dispossessed of their indigenous land base. The fruits of
production will be shared equitably among all Azania's citizens.
All classes of people will be entitled to the fundamental human
rights of education, health care, employment, and to the development of their God-endowed gifts. Women will be accorded dignity

2. The author was involved in a project coordinated by the Center for Ethics
and Social Policy at the Graduate Theological Union in Berkeley in the late eighties
that supported the struggle for native Hawaiian religious rights and opposed the
development of geothermal power on the Big Island that resulted in the partial
denuding of the Puna rainforest.

3. The history and effects of environmental devastation in the U.S. are well
documented in Joseph M. Petulla's *Environmental Protection in the United States:
Industry, Agencies and Environmentalists* (San Francisco: San Francisco Study
Center, 1987), furnishing an illuminative treatment of the need for environmental
restoration and ecological preservation.

4. Azania is the name of the post-apartheid society that members of the Azanian Peoples' Organization and the Pan Africanist Congress use, symbolizing their
hopes and aspirations for a radically new nation. Azania is derived from the word
zang used by early north African traders to refer to southern Africa.

and justice as God's co-creation with men. Most importantly, persons from the working class and the underclass will participate at all high levels of decision-making in the government. Reconciliation between colonizer and colonized will become an existential reality only when the political and economic power that was previously unequally distributed becomes a prerogative and possession of *all* of the people.

Some critics assert that the post-liberation phase of any struggle is the most important period in assessing the legitimacy of people's movements. During the period of rebuilding the new Turtle Island and the new Azania, black theology must continually seek the direction of the Holy Spirit. The mode of transformation undertaken by the liberation movements needs to be assessed in the context of critical ethical reflection, a movement in which all religious communities are called to be decisively involved. The inspiration of the Holy Spirit is pivotal in this regard. The Spirit serves to check brash action in liberation events, where the subconscious internalization of the former oppressor's values may locate themselves in the psychic reconstruction of reality by the formerly oppressed. The sinful proclivity toward demonization of human structures is possible in any society, including the establishment of alternative structures by the oppressed. No situation where people are involved is bereft of human sinfulness.

The assurance of God's redemptive grace functions as a sobering reminder that the Creator is still in control of the world and that ultimately God is responsible for saving and renewing the world in its totality. As much as human beings have been blessed by the Creator with critical consciousness and indelibly stamped by the *imago Dei,* they are still capable of diabolical and egotistical behavior. No human social or economic system of whatever persuasion can be deified or absolutized, since all are provisional and are still subject to God's grace. As instruments of God's Holy Spirit, the black working class and underclass are called to witness to God's reign in liberated societies in the United States and South Africa. Black theology's ultimate allegiance is to the Creator, *Umvelinqangi,*[5] whose creative and re-creative power is manifest in ways of liberation. The oppressed must be led by the dynamism of the Holy Spirit in working in concert for the establishment of authentic community among all Americans and all South Africans that would lead to eventual reconciliation with other nations, with the rest of creation, and with

---

5. This word means "God the Creator" in Xhosa, a major language of South Africa.

the Creator. Then the old Native American Navajo chant can be extolled in unison:

> The soles of its feet, they are beautiful
> Its legs, they are beautiful
> Its body, it is beautiful
> Its chest, it is beautiful
> Its breath, it is beautiful
> Its head-father, it is beautiful
> The Earth is beautiful.[6]

6. Earl Waugh and K. Dad Prithipaul, *Native Religious Traditions,* published for the Canadian Corporation for Studies in Religion, Ontario, 1979, 107–8.

The Tale of Nomabhadi
and the Mbulu-Makhasana

It came about, according to some tale, that a certain village was visited by drought and famine. There were no crops in the fields and very little water in the springs and rivers, and no grass for the cattle and goats. The cattle died in large and small numbers in every homestead until there were none left in the whole village. Then followed the goats. These died one by one until only one she-goat was left. This goat belonged to the home of a beautiful young girl named Nomabhadi, and she and her two brothers fed on its milk. The names of the brothers were Ngubendala, the first-born, and Sihele, the last-born.

As the spell of the drought continued, things became worse and worse. The food stores in the corn-pits were running low, and there was no milk for the young children. To have any soup the people had to boil the skins of the dead domestic animals, cutting off a tiny bit at a time in order that the skins should last as long as possible. When these were finished and the corn-pits gone empty, the children began to die of hunger. They died in twos and threes and fours until the only children left in the whole village were Nomabhadi and her two brothers, and they were saved by the milk of the family goat. This calamity so hit the village that all the grown-ups except Nomabhadi's parents seemed unable to speak. They walked about silently with bowed heads, and the only things that seemed to brighten them at any time was to see Nomabhadi and her brothers running about and to hear their little voices. But Nomabhadi's parents were worried, too. The goat was running dry, and very soon their children might go the way the rest of the village children had gone.

At last, a light shower of rain fell, and Nomabhadi's parents immediately set about getting their hoes ready so that they could plant some corn. They were the only people in the village who had any spirit left in them for such work. The rest were so weak in body and so broken in spirit that they seemed to be looking forward to the day when they would be carried away to the land of the shades to join their children. But when they saw Nomabhadi's parents hoeing their field one morning, all the people of the village took their hoes and went to help them. No one said a word to anyone else during the hoeing. Men and women came and hoed away in the hot sun from morning to sunset, and then they carried their hoes home, to return again the following day and work as hard as ever without speaking.

Nomabhadi's parents felt so grateful to their neighbors that one evening they sat and considered how to show their gratitude. The goat had now gone quite dry and there was no point in keeping it alive any longer. So they agreed that they had better slaughter it and invite all their helpers to a modest feast at the end of the next day's work. This was carried out, and the following morning Nomabhadi's mother stayed home to prepare the feast. At the end of the day's work, all the villagers came and feasted in silence. They then went to their several homes to sleep and rest, so that they could rise early the next morning and then continue the hoeing.

For some days, Nomabhadi's parents fed themselves and their children on the tripe of the goat, and when that was finished, on bits of the skin. Occasionally, the mother produced a tiny bit of dry bread and made all the children share it. It was clear now that the children were starving. Quarrels arose among them at meal time, especially between the two brothers. Ngubendala grumbled because his younger brother got the biggest share of anything they were given. He just would not accept the view that because Sihele was the youngest, he should therefore have more to eat than anyone else in the family.

One morning, after the parents had gone to the fields, Nomabhadi brought out some soup that the mother had left ready for the children to drink as soon as they got up. There was very, very little indeed, but as usual, Sihele had a little more than the others. As soon as the little bowls were put in front of them, Ngubendala looked at his share and looked at his younger brother's. Then he seized his bowl, drank the soup at one gulp and then grabbed his younger brother's. Sihele held on, protesting aloud, and in the struggle all the soup spilled on the ground. In his rage, Ngubendala struck his younger brother on the head with the empty bowl and killed him.

Things had happened so quickly that Nomabhadi hadn't time to come between her brothers. When she saw what had happened, she buried her face in her hands and sobbed. Meanwhile, Ngubendala looked around in alarm, carried his brother's body to the edge of the enclosure, dug a shallow grave, and buried it.

He came back and sat sullenly next to his sister. Then, after a little while he turned around and asked her, "Why are you crying, Nomabhadi?"

Silence.

Again, rather sharply, "Nomabhadi, why are you crying?"

"Because, because I — I am hungry," she replied.

"Did you see anything?"

Silence.

"Nomabhadi, I'm asking you did you see anything?" this time sharply and threateningly.

"N-no! I didn't see anything."

"All right, my sister. Stop crying now."

Ngubendala was sitting in a coiled-up position, his arms rested on his knees crosswise, and his head rested on his arms. He was silent.

Nomabhadi slipped out of the courtyard and walked towards the fields. As she walked she sang sadly:

U-Sihelan' ubulewe	Little Sihele has been killed.
Ngu-Ngubendala	By Ngubendala
Ngu-Ngubendala	By Ngubendala

Suddenly, Ngubendala overtook her and demanded sharply:

"What's that you're singing, Nomabhadi? What's that you're singing?"

Nomabhadi replied, "I'm only singing:

Awu! Awu! Mhm!	O! O! Alas!
Awu! Awu! Awu!	O! O! Alas!

"Oh, good! Go on then, my sister."

Nomabhadi went on a little, and then sang her sad song again. Ngubendala, who had been following her at some distance, overtook her again and wanted to know what she was singing, and again she told him she was only singing: *"Awu! Awu! Mhm!"* Again Ngubendala was satisfied and allowed her to proceed. This went on for a long time and Ngubendala decided to go back home.

As Nomabhadi drew nearer and nearer, her voice reached the hoers in the field. Without saying a word to one another, they stopped hoeing and strained their ears to catch the words of her song. The first one to catch the words exclaimed: "Do you hear what she sings? Ngubendala has killed his younger brother!"

Thereupon, the one next to him exclaimed in horror, *"Hayi, suka!"* (Oh, no!) and struck his neighbor dead with his hoe.

The rest listened again, and then a second hearer exclaimed, "Yes! She says Ngubendala has killed his younger brother!" He met the same fate as the first reporter from the hoer next to him. This went on and on. Each one who caught the words and reported was killed by the one next to him. Man killed woman and woman killed man in this way until only Nomabhadi's parents were left to hear the whole story.

As soon as Nomabhadi had finished telling them what had happened, they shouldered their hoes and went home without saying a word. Nomabhadi followed behind, still sobbing. On reaching home, the parents caught Ngubendala, killed him and buried him next to his brother without saying a word to him or to each other.

The mother then took out a piece of dry bread—the last piece of food they had in the house—and gave it to her daughter.

"My child," she said, "If you remain in this village any longer, you will die of hunger. You've been to my brother's village over yonder mountains many times, and you can get there alone easily, can't you?"

"Yes, I can, mother."

"Good! Now as you know very well, they have plenty to eat over there because they have plenty of rain. My brother has more cows, more goats, more corn, more pumpkins than anyone else in his village. He has many children. They are healthy and happy and kind. You will play with them the whole day. My brother's wife is a very kind person. She will look very well after you. If you go at once, you'll reach there before nightfall. When you feel hungry, just eat a little of your bread, and don't wander off your way to look for berries in the thicket."

As her parents embraced her, Nomabhadi began to sob again.

"Don't cry now, my child," said the mother, trying to look cheerful. "If you cry along the way, the Mbulu will hear you, overtake you and rob you of your bread. Remember, you are to look straight ahead all the time. Don't look to the right or to the left. Above all, my child, don't look back. Do you hear? Don't look back at all!"

Nomabhadi set out for her mother's brother's village. It was a fairly long stretch to the foot of the mountains, but she walked out bravely and took the winding path up the slope steadily. But before she disappeared over the ridge, the desire to take one last look at her old home was too strong. She looked back. What she saw made her cry out in pain. The whole homestead was in flames. She knew at once what this meant. Her parents had burned everything in the courtyard, set fire to each and every one of the smaller huts, and then shut themselves in their own great hut and set fire to it from the inside. She would never see her father and mother again.

As she turned to resume her journey, she remembered her mother's warning that she was not to cry, and she quickly checked her sobs. But her first cry of pain had been heard, for she heard a strange voice calling to her in a lisp, "Sister! Sister! Why are you crying? Wait for me."

With a start, Nomabhadi wiped away her tears and, before she knew what she was doing, she had looked left and right to see where the voice was coming from. A strange creature had just emerged from the thicket and was running to overtake her. It was half-human, half-beast. It was walking on its hindlimbs but could not hold its body up. Its body was wrapped in the skin of some animal resembling the baboon, but much bigger. What she could see of its face was human, but all the facial bones were sticking out and the cheeks were hollow, as if they had been sucked in. Its body was hard and dry, as if drained of all blood and water. Its hands were coarse and bony, and its nails were long and ugly. It had a long, lively tail that contrasted with the tail of the baboon-like animal whose skin this creature was wearing.

"Don't be afraid of me," it said as it overtook her. "I am your sister. Stop crying and tell me your name."

Nomabhadi had heard descriptions of the Mbulu many times, and the appearance of this creature, its manner of speech, and its voice tallied so well with these descriptions that she knew at once that this was one. But this Mbulu was kind and called her "sister." So why should she fear it?

"My name is Nomabhadi," she replied, trying to smile.

"Nomabhadi, Nomabhadi," the Mbulu said repeatedly. "Its a nice name, a very nice name indeed."

"And what's *your* name?" asked Nomabhadi.

"Oh, just call me 'sister.' I'll tell you what. Let's just call each other 'sister.' I'll call you 'sister' too, though I like the name Nomabhadi very much. Nomabhadi, Nomabhadi." The Mbulu repeated the name over and over again as they went along, but all the time with the lisp that Nomabhadi had already noted.

Then the Mbulu noticed the small bundle on Nomabhadi's head.

"Sister," it called, "what have you got in that bundle? Is there any bread or meat? I'm very hungry. I haven't had anything to eat for many, many days."

There could be no doubt that this was true, and Nomabhadi, knowing what it was to be hungry and used to sharing with others, steadily replied, "Oh, yes, I have some bread, sister. It's little enough, but I'll share it with you."

But as soon as the bread was produced, the Mbulu stretched out its bony hand greedily and protested, "No, sister, this is too small to share. I'm sure you can't be as hungry as I am."

"It's all right, my sister. You can have it all." And she handed it over.

The Mbulu grabbed it, devoured it greedily and noisily and disappeared in the thicket without even thanking her. Nomabhadi had seen many a hungry child grab greedily at any kind of food it came across in her famished village, but she had never seen anything so disgusting. As she went on her way, she began to feel the pangs of hunger, and she remembered how her mother had warned her about the Mbulu. She did not cry, but as she went, she sang sadly:

Wayetshil' umama	My mother did warn me
Mpanga-mpa!	*Mpanga-mpa!*
Wayetshil' umama	My mother did warn me
Mpanga-mpa!	*Mpanga-mpa!*
Ndosukelwa yimbulu	That a Mbulu would chase me
Mpanga-mpa!	*Mpanga-mpa!*
Ihluth' isonka sami	And rob me of my bread
Mpanga-mpa!	*Mpanga-mpa!*

Suddenly, she became aware that she was surrounded by beauty. She was traveling through forestland. It was a long time since she had heard so many little birds twittering and chirping, or even so many beautiful, bright-colored butterflies flying from one beautiful flower to another. She forgot her mother's warning altogether and gazed with delight at this gay new world. Her eye was arrested by one particularly bright-colored butterfly that crossed her path and landed on what first seemed to be a shrub but turned out, to her delight, to be *msobosobo* (a sweet tasting fruit). Screaming with excitement, she ran across the road, grabbed the plant by its stem and pulled it out by its roots, and then went on her way, plucking the berries and eating them so greedily that in a short while not only her tongue but also her lips and cheeks were stained purple by the sweet juice of her favorite msobosobo.

"Sister! Sister!" came a voice from the thicket. "Here I am again. Oh, don't eat all the berries before I come. Leave some for me."

It was the Mbulu, as gaunt and greedy as ever. Nomabhadi was very hungry now and therefore not prepared to give up all her *msobosobo* to this creature. But on catching up with her, the Mbulu protested, "Oh, you've almost finished it" and, wrenching the plant from her hands, it devoured the *msobosobo* without even plucking the fruit.

This time the Mbulu did not run back to the thicket but went along with her, gazing in admiration at her clothes. After some time it asked her to tell all about herself, her people, her village and its people. Nomabhadi told the story of her life fully, and the Mbulu paid the closest attention to every little detail. When she had finished, the Mbulu seemed deeply moved.

"I weep for you, my sister," it said, covering its face with its hands as people do when they weep. "I must go along with you so that no harm may befall you. I'll take you right into your mother's people's house."

Nomabhadi felt very thankful, for indeed the Mbulu proved a wonderful traveling companion. It taught her many games which they played together as they traveled, and she found these so amusing that she forgot her hunger and fatigue.

They came to a river.

"I'll teach you another game, sister," said the Mbulu. "We're going to compete. Lets see which one of us will be able to get to the other bank of the river without getting any part of her body wet. You hop from one stone to another, like this, like this. Whoever touches the water before reaching the other bank has to take off her clothes and bathe her whole body. Do you think you can try?"

"I've crossed our river many times like that without getting wet," said Nomabhadi brightly, "and I'm sure I'll reach the other bank of this one quite dry."

"You lead the way, my sister," said the Mbulu, smiling.

As it followed her into the water, the Mbulu felt quite sure that Nomabhadi would miss her footing, by jumping too short or too long, before reaching the other bank. But Nomabhadi hopped from one flat rock to another with such skill that the Mbulu realized that she was going to reach the other bank quite dry. So, just as she made the last rock before reaching the bank, it dipped its tail in the water and splashed it on her legs.

"You've touched the water!" it shouted. "Look at your legs! Come, take off your clothes and bathe your whole body."

Nomabhadi looked at her legs and, true enough, they were wet. She was greatly puzzled at this, because she was quite sure that she had not touched the water at all, but as she could not explain how her legs got wet, she decided not to argue. She was not at all averse to bathing as such. She loved bathing and was a good swimmer. Quickly she took off her clothes and, with only her *nkciyo* (waist-apron) on, she plunged into the deepest part of the river, swimming delightfully first from one bank to the other, then downstream, upstream, now face down, now on her back. It was most refreshing.

Meanwhile, the Mbulu was watching her closely, and as soon as it noticed that she was really carried away by the rhythm of her own swimming, it threw off its covering, wound its tail round its waist and put on Nomabhadi's clothes. The swimmer did not notice this until the Mbulu called out, "Come out now, sister. It's time to go."

Looking up and seeing the Mbulu in her clothes, Nomabhadi was horrified, and she swam quickly up the bank.

"My clothes, please! My clothes!" she said, rather curtly.

"Oh, just a little, sister," said the Mbulu. "I'm only trying them on."

"No! I want my clothes. Take them off at once."

"Oh how pretty I look in these clothes," said the Mbulu, paying no heed to Nomabhadi but gazing in admiration at its own image in the water. Then it turned and looked at her appealingly and said, "Sister, don't be so unkind to me. I've been very kind to you, coming with you all this way and teaching you delightful games. I'm not going to run away in your clothes. I'm not asking you to give them to me to keep either. I just want to walk a little distance in them and feel how it is to walk in pretty clothes. I've never had such clothes. My parents are poor. It will make me happy to be in nice clothes for once. Come, sister, let me wrap you in my garment and we'll continue our journey."

And without waiting for a reply, the Mbulu picked up its garment and proceeded to wrap Nomabhadi in it, covering her whole body except the eyes and forearms and lower parts of the legs and knotting it carefully.

As they continued their journey, the Mbulu kept Nomabhadi's mind away from the new situation by teaching her one game after another, and by the time they reached the river, she was quite happy again. But when she reminded the Mbulu about her clothes, it said, "Wait until we cross the third and last river, sister. It's not far."

When they reached the last river, they were in full view of Nomabhadi's mother's people's house.

"Give me my clothes quickly," she said. "My mother's people mustn't see me dressed in this thing of yours." And in her impatience she tried to take it off. But it was so cunningly knotted at so many points that she could not undo any of the knots.

"But your mother's people's home is not in sight yet?"

"Yes, it is."

"Which one is it?"

"That one over there." And she pointed it out.

"That big one with many beautiful huts fenced in with wood? And do all those fat cattle and goats belong to your mother's brother?"

"Yes," replied Nomabhadi with pride. "You can come with me. I'll tell them you've been very kind to me. They'll give you meat, milk, bread, and pumpkin, and you'll be full before you leave. My mother's people are very generous. They'll even give you a leg of mutton to carry home to your mother, because you've been so kind to me."

"All right, sister. I'll come with you. But just let me wear these pretty clothes a little longer. Do you see that big ant-heap over there? I'll give you your clothes when we reach it."

So they went on. But when they reached the tree, Nomabhadi was already struggling impatiently to get the loathsome garment off her body, but she could not undo the knots. Then suddenly the Mbulu turned round, and, with the most savage look in its face it said, "Look here! From this moment onwards, I am Nomabhadi and you are *Msila-wanja* my dog. These are my mother's people. If you ever open your mouth in this house, I'll kill you."

Nomabhadi was so terrified by the look on the Mbulu's face that it took her a little time to take in what was happening, and when she did, the Mbulu was inside the enclosure and making for the Great Hut. She caught up with it near the door. It turned around to give her another savage look to warn her, and then knocked at the door.

"Greetings, *malume* (uncle)!" it said to the head of the house. "Greetings *malumekazi*" (feminine of malume), this to the mistress of the house. "Why? Don't you know me? I'm Nomabhadi, your sister's daughter."

The people were stunned. They had heard accounts of the happenings in Nomabhadi's home village, but they had never thought that their sister's child would be in such a state. Nomabhadi, once so full and beautiful, now so emaciated and ugly! Nomabhadi's voice, once so sweet and refined, now so husky and coarse! Nomabhadi's whole personality, once so pleasant, now so distasteful! A curse must have come upon her home village. And this ugly creature that followed her into the house! What was it?

The Mbulu glanced over its shoulder to give Nomabhadi a warning look and then proceeded to tell the story of Nomabhadi's home village to the last detail.

"I myself," concluded the Mbulu, "was very ill, so ill that for many moons after I recovered I was unable to speak. That's why I can't speak properly now. The muscles of my tongue are stiff and the tongue itself feels shorter."

After hearing what the "poor child" had gone through, the people could understand why she should be in such a state.

"And your companion? Who is she?" asked the head of the house, pointing to Nomabhadi.

"Companion!" exclaimed the Mbulu with a coarse laugh. "No, *malume*, this is only a strange animal that overtook me on my way here. I don't know what animal it is, but it's very intelligent and understands me when I speak to it. I gave all my food to it because it was very hungry, and after that it kept on following me, and so I decided to keep it as my dog and have given it the name *Msila-wanja* (dog's tail) because of its tail."

By this time, the evening meal was ready. The people were disgusted by the "niece's" manner of eating. Her skinny hands went from one dish to another as if she feared someone would snatch the food away from her. She grabbed huge chunks of meat, biting off large pieces and chewing noisily, crunching the bones. She grabbed the bowl of *amasi* (curds) and instead of filling her cup from it, she held the bowl between her hands and drank noisily out of it.

Meanwhile, Nomabhadi, who had been ordered to have her scraps of food outside the hut, had made friends with the dogs. She had given all the scraps to the dogs, for she felt she would rather die of hunger than eat scraps in her own mother's brother's house while the Mbulu enjoyed all the privileges that were rightfully hers. She spent that night in the company of the dogs, her only friends in this great house.

The following morning, the girls of the house had to go to the fields and stay there the whole day keeping the birds away from the corn. The Mbulu, in order to keep Nomabhadi as far away from her *malume* and *malumekazi* as possible, ordered her to go and help the girls. Ordinarily, the girls took turns in their work. One would take her position in the middle of the field and the rest would sit or stand in a group outside the field, but in such a position that they could see the birds coming and tell the one in the middle of the field which way to go to scare them away. They enjoyed this occupation because it offered them plenty of time to play in the open air. So they used to carry plenty of food with them, eat when they felt like doing so, play games, lounge about and so on.

On this occasion things were better than ever, for they had *Msila-wanja* with them, and they would make her take the position in the middle of the field and remain there the whole day while they enjoyed themselves on the slope, only now and again calling out to the "dog," *"Nanzo, Msila-wanja"* (There they come, *Msila-wanja!*).

Whereupon Nomabhadi would run across the field, waving her long stick and shouting:

Tayi! Tayi bo!	Tayi! Tayi bo!
Ezo ntaka sidl' amabele	Three birds are eating my
Noko angemalume wenene	mother's brother's corn,
Kuba mna se ndingumsila-	No mother's brother in truth
wanja,	For today I am a mere *msila-wanja*
Kanti eneneni ndandingu	Whereas in truth I was
Nomabhadi	Nomabhadi.

This then was Nomabhadi's occupation on her first day with her mother's people while the Mbulu gobbled and gobbled at the house. She had to run from one end of the field to the other according to the directions of the guard on the slope above the cornfields.

By midday she could not bear the Mbulu's garment any more. It was suffocating her. So she sat down, sought all the knots so cunningly tied by the Mbulu, untied them and hung it on a tree to scare the birds away. Then with nothing on except her *nkciya,* she went to a stream at the edge of the cornfield and bathed.

On returning to her position in the field, she did not feel inclined to put on the Mbulu's garment again. She picked up the long stick that she had been using to scare the birds, returned to the bank of the stream and sat on a rock. The bathing had certainly refreshed her, but it also made her feel very hungry. What was she to do? She would never, never live on scraps in her own mother's brother's house. She had thrown away the scraps that the other girls had given her when they ordered her to take up her position in the field. She would rather die than pick up those scraps again. In despair she sang:

Wayetshil' umama	My mother did warn
Mpanga-mpa!	*Mpanga-mpa!*
Wayetshil' umama	My mother did warn
Mpanga-mpa!	*Mpanga-mpa!*
Ndosukelwa yimbulu	That a Mbulu would chase me
Mpanga-mpa!	*Mpanga-mpa!*
Ihluth' isonka sami	And take away my bread
Mpanga-mpa!	*Mpanga-mpa!*

"If only I had been strong enough not to look back to my old home before climbing that hill, I would never have cried out, and the Mbulu would never have known that I was there. And now my weakness has brought so many troubles upon me. The Mbulu robbed me not only of the last piece of bread my mother gave me but also of my clothes and my rightful place with my mother's people. This creature has fooled me all the way, calling me sister, begging for food, borrowing my clothes. I could bear all this. But to rob me of my name and to say to my own mother's people that I am its dog! I the Mbulu's dog! My own mother's people to treat me like a dog — the Mbulu's dog! I'd rather die than bear this any longer!"

She sang again:

Gantshi! Gantshi-ntshi!	*Gantshi! Gantshi-ntshi!*
Yimbulukazana	It's a little female Mbulu!
Gantshi! Gantshi-ntshi	*Gantshi! Gantshi-ntshi!*
Yimbulukazana!	It's a little female Mbulu!
Ndenzwe sidengazana, yoho!	A fool she made of me, *yoho!*
Yimbulukazana	That little female Mbulu!
Ndenziwe sidengazana, yoho	A fool she made of me, *yoho!*
Yimbulukazana!	That little female Mbulu!

Then she seized the scaring-stick and struck the ground hard with it, calling out aloud: "Open, O Earth, and swallow me, for I've no mother and father!" Thereupon the ground began to shake where she had struck it, then it opened, and behold! There were the shades of her parents standing in an open grave. They had brought her plenty of food, clothes, and beautiful ornaments, and without saying a word, they held these up to their daughter. She received them with great joy, first the food, which she laid aside on the green grass, and then the clothes and ornaments, which she put on immediately. Then she settled down to eat while the shades of her parents watched silently.

As soon as she had finished eating, the shades held up their arms, indicating that everything was to be handed back to them. Nomabhadi took off her clothes and ornaments, packed them and handed them back to the shades together with the mats and bowls and cups in which the food had been served to her. Then the shades vanished and the grave closed and everything was as it had been before.

This made Nomabhadi very happy. She no longer wished to die, for now she knew that her parents wanted her to live. If they had wanted her to die, they would have received her into the open grave and carried her to the land of the shades. She knew also that it was their wish that she should continue wearing the Mbulu's garment, otherwise they wouldn't have taken those beautiful clothes and ornaments back to the land of the shades. She would live! She would live! And all this would be corrected sooner or later. She ran back to her post and put on the Mbulu's garment.

"It's time to go home, *Msila-wanja!*" shouted one of the girls on guard. For the first time, the name *Msila-wanja* amused rather than hurt Nomabhadi. She smiled, collected her belongings and went back to the house as calmly as if nothing had happened and as unobtrusively as was expected of her in her position as *Msila-wanja.*

In her misery that afternoon, Nomabhadi had been quite forgetful of her surroundings, forgetful of her cousins on guard, forgetful of the women who were working in the neighboring fields. Her songs had not been heard by her cousins, because these girls had been running about, laughing and shouting the whole day. But the women in the neighboring fields had heard her songs and wondered, for they had never heard such a beautiful voice in that neighborhood. They could not catch the words, but they could make out that the songs were full of meaning. They had gone on working, hoping that sooner or later the singer would emerge from the stream, but the only living thing that came out of the fields a little later was the *msila-wanja* about whom the whole village had heard by now.

On the following day, Nomabhadi went to the fields again. Early in the afternoon she did exactly what she had done on the previous day, throwing off the Mbulu's garment, bathing, singing her songs and striking the ground with her scaring-stick. This time the village women came softly, each from her field, listened to the beautiful singing and catching and noting every word. They saw the ground opening and the food and clothes coming out of the earth, but they did not see the shades. Each one of them was stricken with fear and concluded that something very deep was happening.

That night, the women of the village came together to discuss the situation, for what they had seen was such a wonderful thing that each one of them wanted to know if the others had seen exactly what she had seen. When they were satisfied that they had all seen the same thing, they decided to tell Nomabhadi's mother's people that same night.

Her mother's brother was astounded when he heard the story. He immediately called his most trusted neighbor and made the women repeat the story in his presence. Then they decided that this matter must not be known to anyone outside of the Great Hut until the men had satisfied themselves that there really were such goings-on in the fields. The women were asked not to go anywhere near the stream on the following day.

Early the next morning, the head of the house and his trusted neighbor went to hide themselves near the spot as described by the women and waited to see what would happen. Things happened exactly as on the previous two days. The men watched until everything was over, and just as Nomabhadi was putting on the Mbulu's garment, they came out of their hiding place. Her mother's brother immediately took the garment off her body, handed it to his neighbor and, without saying a word, took his sister's child into his arms and carried her tenderly into his house. The trusted neighbor followed with the Mbulu's garment. Without being seen by any of the people of the house, they took Nomabhadi into a private hut and then called the mistress of the house to come and hear the story. Then for the first time they heard the voice of their true *mtshana* (sister's child) who told them all that had happened to her.

When they heard the story, they all agreed that this evil must be exposed and destroyed in the presence of all their neighbors. They knew the habits of the Mbulu. Its tail could not resist sour corn and milk. The test on sour corn would be carried out the same night. The "Thing" would be made to sleep in a hut where there was sour corn, and some elderly women would spend the night in that same hut and watch what happened. If the results pointed out that this was really a Mbulu, they would carry out the milk test and destroy the "Thing" nearby. Meanwhile, everybody was to continue being as kind and indulgent to the Mbulu as ever, so that it would not suspect anything.

So the mistress of the house saw to it that a hut was prepared for the Mbulu and three elderly women. Then, unknown to the girls who prepared the hut, she herself put some sour corn in a hidden place outside. After the evening meal, the Mbulu was told that since she was of marriageable age and would soon be asked for by one of the wealthy families in the village, it was necessary that she should spend at least one night in the exclusive company of three elderly women who would tell her all she had to know about marriage and married life.

When the Mbulu entered the hut, she found the three elderly women there. These had been warned strictly that at least one of them at a time must be awake throughout the night in order that every little thing that happened might be noted. So when the Mbulu came in, they had already decided to take turns in watching. For some time they spoke freely and openly about marriage. But they noticed that the Mbulu was not paying attention to their teaching. Instead, it kept on adjusting its skirt. The women noted this and exchanged significant glances. The tail of the Mbulu had smelled the sour corn and was unfolding itself. The Mbulu was anxious that the light be put out partly because it feared that its restlessness would be detected and suspected, and partly because it wanted these women to fall asleep so that its tail could trace the sour corn. This suited the women, and they put out the light at once and very soon they pretended to snore. Then the tail became very lively, brushing the faces of the women as it flew all around the hut hunting for the sour corn. None of the women slept a wink that night. At one time one of them jumped up and called out, "What's this brushing against my face? I can't sleep at all!" Whereupon the Mbulu answered immediately, "It must be a rat, grandma! It must be a rat! Please lie down and sleep." Then it folded its tail and wound its waist as tightly as it could so that there should be no movement until the old woman had fallen asleep. But the tail had got completely out of control. It unwound itself immediately and made such a noise that the women could no longer pretend to be asleep.

"There's evil in this house!" said the shrewdest of them. "Unless the head of this family does something at once, this niece of his will die unmarried. Why is it that we heard such noises in this hut as soon as preparations begin for our marriage? My child, you are in danger. We must tell your *malume* to take steps at once to avert the evil that is threatening you."

The Mbulu was flattered by this, and when the elderly women left the hut at daybreak, it felt relieved because it thought they were on its side, and it folded its tail and fell asleep.

It was awakened by an announcement that was shouted at every door just a little after sunrise. The announcement was that it had been discovered that there was an evil person in the house; that the head of the family had therefore invited the whole village to come and see him and the clean people of the house expose the evil person: that no one was to leave the house without the permission of the head; that a deep pit was at that very moment being dug and a bowl of milk was going to be put at the bottom of this pit; that every single person who had spent the previous night in this house was going to be made to jump over this pit, and the evil one would be exposed by the clean milk at the bottom; that the head of the house was going to slaughter an ox so that the clean people of the village might not leave his house hungry after his house had been cleansed of evil.

The Mbulu was horrified at this announcement, so horrified that for once it did not go to the cooking hut first thing in the morning to look for food. It went from one end of the household to the other to see if there was no way of escape. But whichever way it turned, there was a young man on guard who told it that no one was to leave the house. In despair it went into the pumpkin garden, sat on a flat rock, unwound its tail and began to plead with it to break it off.

"Oh, my tail! My beautiful tail! Can you be unkind to me after I have done so many good things for you? Why won't you break off? I beg you, my tail, to break off just for today. I am going to hide you here so that no one may find you, and I promise you as soon as this jumping is over, I shall return here, pick you up and restore you to your place. Help me! Please help me, my beautiful tail!"

Because the tail would not break off on its own, the Mbulu tried to bite it off, but became so sore that it had to give it up. Then it found a stone, laid the tail flat on the rock on which it was sitting, and tried to break the tail by hitting it with the stone in its hand, but it could not summon up courage to hit hard enough. After each blow it jumped up writhing with pain and exclaimed, *"Shu! Shu! Shu!"* At last it had to give up this also. So the only thing the Mbulu could do was to wind its tail around its waist and fasten it tighter than ever before. This was also very sore, but it had to be done.

The villagers arrived in the early afternoon, and the whole household was ordered to report to the pit. *Msila-wanja* was there too, covered with the Mbulu's garment. When the Mbulu saw her, it drew the attention of the head of the house to her, protesting that a mere dog could not compete with people.

"It is my order," said the head of the house and turned away.

Then all those who had spent the previous night in this house were made to stand in a line. The head and the mistress of the house were in this line too, and so were the elderly women who had spent the night in the company of the Mbulu. The trusted neighbor was in charge of affairs, while the most reliable of his sons took command of the guard to see that no one who had spent the night in that house escaped the test. Each person was allowed to take any position in the line of jumpers. The Mbulu chose to be right at the back, in the hope that by some lucky chance some other person might be exposed by the milk before its turn came. *Msila-wanja* was somewhere in the middle.

Then one by one the people of the household jumped over the pit while the rest of the villagers watched. One after another they cleared the pit until the Mbulu was left. Summoning up its courage, the creature took a wild leap, reckoning that it might reach the other side before the tail betrayed it. But the tail broke loose right in the air, and shot straight down to the center of the milk bowl in the pit, dragging the Mbulu down with it. Immediately some men, who had been given orders beforehand, quickly filled the pit with earth and buried the Mbulu alive. The head of the house removed the hateful garment from his niece and burned it over the Mbulu's grave.

A big fat ox had been driven into the cattle fold before the test, and now the head of the house ordered that as his house had been cleansed of evil, this ox must be slaughtered in honor of his sister's daughter. By the time the ox had been flayed and the meat prepared for the feast, Nomabhadi was dressed in beautiful clothes and garments. Before the feasting, her malumekazi brought her out of the girl's hut, and her malume presented her to the villagers, relating her whole story and thanking those neighbors' wives who had heard her song and told him what they had heard and seen.

From that moment, Nomabhadi took her rightful place in the house of her mother's people and became very happy. Her body filled up quickly, her pleasant personality was restored, and she developed into a beautiful young woman.

It soon became known throughout the village that the trusted neighbor had visited Nomabhadi's uncle to make a request that she become his daughter-in-law and the wife of his handsome son, but that this request would not be considered until Nomabhadi had undergone her initiation.

So one day Nomabhadi was removed to a secluded hut. Here she was going to be in the company of elderly women who would teach her all the things that a girl must know about marriage and married life before she goes into it. They would also bathe her with the sweet-scented *mthombothi* and feed her well, so that at the end of the period of seclusion she would be refined and beautiful in body as well as in spirit. During the period of seclusion she would be known as the *ntonjane*. She might not leave her hut until the period was over, but other women might visit her. The instructresses, on the other hand, could leave the hut occasionally and go to other parts of the household.

On the evening of the first day of seclusion, Nomabhadi was lying peacefully and calmly in her hut when she suddenly heard a "thud-thud" coming toward the hut. She listened wondering, and then she heard a faint voice calling, "*Ntonjane,* who are you with in there?"

"I'm alone," she replied.

Thereupon a huge melon came leaping into the hut.

"I'm going to kill you!" shouted the melon.

"You'll never kill me!" shouted Nomabhadi, leaping to her feet. For in the few words uttered by the melon she had detected the lisp of the Mbulu!

She had hardly uttered her defiant reply when the melon made a leap at her face, hitting her so hard that she fell on her back and all but bumped her head against the wall. But on a twinkling she was on her feet again, determined to fight back. When the melon flung itself at her a second time, she caught it and threw it hard on the ground, trying to crush it. Nothing happened to the melon. But apparently it sensed that someone was approaching, for instead of charging a third time it made for the door.

"You'll never kill me. Never!" shouted Nomabhadi, panting but determined.

"Who are you talking to?" asked one of the elderly women returning. She was alarmed to find the *ntonjane* on her feet agitated, and shouting to the air, when she should have been lying calm and quiet on her bed of reeds behind the curtain. Had something gone wrong with the *ntonjane's* mind, she wondered?

When she heard Nomabhadi's story, the old woman was troubled.

"Something must be done at once" she said quietly. "It is clear that the evil has not been destroyed altogether. I must see your *malume* at once. But I can't leave you alone again. If you had come to any harm just now, all of us who are looking after you would have been in trouble."

"You can leave me alone. I am sure I'll come to no harm. That thing will never kill me. Never!"

"No, my child's child. These things are not done that way. It is your mother's people, your *malume*, who must rid you of this thing."

The old woman went to the doorway, called one of the girls, and ordered her to tell one of the women to come at once. As soon as this woman came, the elderly woman went to see the head of the house, leaving Nomabhadi to tell what had just happened.

It was only when the elderly woman reported this incident that it became known, through the young boys in the house, that a wild melon plant had sprung out of the Mbulu's grave during the last few days. As soon as he heard this, the head of the house took an ax, went to examine the spot, and true enough, there was a wild melon plant and a huge melon attached to the stem. He broke off the stem, chopped the melon to pieces and left it there for the animals to eat overnight.

At daybreak, he went to the spot expecting to find the melon gone. But far from being eaten by the animals, the melon had gathered together overnight and became one solid mass once again attached to the stem. He went straight back to the house, took a firebrand from the hearth, collected some firewood and returned to the Mbulu's grave. He pulled out the wild melon at its roots, chopped the stem, the leaves and the melon into tiny pieces. Then he made a big fire on exactly the same spot where he had burned the garment, and he burned the melon, seeing to it that every tiny bit, whether root or pip was reduced to ashes. Then he brought some soil and covered everything.

This was the last heard of the Mbulu. The women were now able to go ahead with the purification rites that Nomabhadi had to undergo, and at the end of the set period, she came out of the hut lovelier than ever. The whole village turned up at the great feast held in her honor on the day of her coming out, and there was singing and dancing by all people according to their age groups.

Soon after this, the trusted neighbor's request was listened to, and the marriage negotiations went apace. Then one day, when the moon was full for the third time after her coming out, Nomabhadi set out for her new home, accompanied by a very large bridal party that carried presents for her in-laws, and amid great rejoicing, she was given in marriage to the handsome son of the trusted friend of her mother's brother.

Statistics Concerning Black People and Low-Income Groups

A. Health Status: 1980[1]	*blacks*	*whites*
Mortality rate	blacks 37% higher than whites	
Mortality rate of women	blacks 37.8% higher than whites	
Male homicide (per 100,000 population)	66.6	10.9
Poverty rate (%)	32.5	10.2
Poor people on Medicaid (%)	25.1	14.7

B. Poverty Conditions: 1983–84[2]	*blacks*	*whites*
Families living in poverty (%)	33.8	11.5
Women under 16 living in poverty (%)	49.2	17.5
Women 22–44 years living in poverty (%)	31.5	11.1
Women 65 years and older living in poverty (%)	35.6	13.1
Poverty in the South (%)	33.6	12
Poverty in the Northeast	33.2	10.7
Children living in poverty (1986) (%)	42.7	15.3

1. Statistics compiled from the U.S. Bureau of Statistics, 1980–84.
2. Statistics compiled from U.S. Bureau of Statistics, 1983–84.

C. Income Levels: 1984[3]

	blacks	whites
Median income	$15,432	$27,686
Under $10,000 (%)	34	11.9
$25,000-34,999 (%)	13.1	19.8
$35,000-49,999 (%)	10.5	19.4
$50,000 and over (%)	5.8	16.9

Income Levels: 1986

	blacks	whites
Median income	$17,604	$30,809
Under $5,000 (%)	14	3.5
$5,000-$9,999 (%)	16.2	6.7
$10,000-$15,000 (%)	13.8	9
$20,000-24,999 (%)	9.6	9.9
$50,000 and over (%)	22.1	8.7

The top 5% of white earners earned 16.8% of the U.S. national income. The top 5% of black earners took 18% of overall black income.[4]

D. Average Household Net Worth: 1986

	blacks	whites
	$3,397	$39,135

E. College Education and Income

	blacks	whites
Percentage of families earning $50,000 or more and earners who had four years or more of college	4.6	15

F. Infant Mortality: 1985–86

	blacks	whites
Deaths per 1,000 births	18.2	9.3
Fetal deaths per 1,000 births	11.3	7.0
Maternal deaths per 1,000	20.4	5.2
Babies born low-weight (%)	12.4	5.6
Prenatal care during first trimester (%)	61.8	79.4

G. Births to Unmarried/Teenage Mothers: 1985

	blacks	whites
Births to unmarried mothers (%)	60.1	22
Births to teenage mothers (%)	23	10.8

H. Unemployment: 1986

	blacks	whites
16–19 years old (%)	39.3	15.6
20–24 years old (%)	24.1	8.7

---

3. Statistics compiled from U.S. Department of Commerce.
4. Statistics compiled from U.S. Bureau of Statistics.

I. Housing: 1986

	blacks	whites
Owner occupied (%)	44.5	66.5

J. Jail Inmates: 1978–86[5]

	blacks	whites
Average number of inmates	98,800	138,355
Federal and state prisons (1985)	227,137	260,847
Under sentence of death	775[6]	1,006

5. Statistics compiled from U.S. Bureau of Justice, 1978–86
6. Including others.

Appendix C

More Recent Statistics Concerning Black People and Low-Income Groups[1]

A. Health Status: 1990	blacks	whites
Death rate for male homicide and legal intervention per 100,000 resident population, age adjusted[2]	68.7	8.9
Life expectancy for females	74.3	79.7
Life expectancy for males	65.6	73.0
Maternal deaths (per 1000 births)	19.1	5.4
Fetal deaths per 1000 births	N/A	6.4
Neonatal deaths	10.9	4.9
Low weight births (%)	13.3	5.7
Death by heart disease (age adjusted for both sexes per 100,000 population)	213.5	146.9
Total death rate (age adjusted for both sexes in each specific group per 100,000 population)	789.2	492.8
Male homicide (in thousands)	12.1	12.2
Male homicide death rate (per 100,000 population in specific group)	69.2	9.0
Male homicide victims (1990) (per 100,000 population)	9,981	9,147
Female homicide death rate (per 100,000 population)	2.8	13.5

---

1. U.S Bureau of the Census, *Statistical Abstract of the United States, 1993*, 113th edition, Washington, D.C., 1993.

2. National Center for Health Statistics, *Health United States, 1992*, Public Health Service, Hyattsville, Maryland, 1993.

	blacks	*whites*
Firearm mortality among children, youth and young adults (25 to 34 year old males per 100,000 population)	108.5	27.8
Medicare recipients (1991)		
Below poverty level (% of total population)	60.9	41.2
Above poverty level (% of total population)	9.7	3.9
Health insurance coverage (%) 1987–89, government or private	60.2	75.8

B. Poverty Conditions: 1991	*blacks*	*whites*
Persons below poverty level (in millions)	10.2	23.7
Children below poverty level (in thousands)	4,637	8,316
Percent of children below poverty level	45.6	16.1
Persons under 16 years below poverty level (in thousands)	4,375	8,135
Persons 22–44 years below poverty level (in thousands)	2,878	7,399
Persons 65 years old below poverty level (in thousands)	880	2,802
Persons below poverty level in the South (in thousands)	5,716	7,837
Poverty rate: 1989 (%)	29.5	9.8

C. Wealth and Income Levels: 1991	*blacks*	*whites*
Median income	$18,807	$31,569
Family net worth (percent of families owning selected non-financial assets)	70.0	93.2
Earnings under $10,000 (%)	30.8	12.8
Earnings $25,000–$34,999 (%)	13.8	15.4
Earnings $35,000–$49,999 (%)	13.4	17.9
Earnings $75,000 and over (%)	3.7	11.2
Median family income	$22,203	$38,229
Median non-family income	$12,202	$18,461

D. Family Net Worth	*blacks*	*whites*
Mean of net worth by selected characteristics (in thousands) (of constant 1989 dollars)	45.9	203.8

E. College Education: 1992

	blacks	whites
Female persons completed 4 years of high school or more (%)	68.2	80.7
Male persons completed 4 years of high school or more (%)	67.0	81.1
Female persons completed 4 years of college or more (%)	12.0	19.1
Male persons completed 4 years of college or more (%)	11.9	25.2
Persons with a bachelors degree (% of population)	8.3	14.6
Persons with an advanced degree (% of population)	3.6	7.5
Persons earning doctorates (in thousands) (1990)	34.0	956.0
Mean monthly income with a bachelors degree (1990)	$2002	$2552
Mean monthly income with a masters degree	$2786	$3248

F. Births to Unmarried Women: 1990

	blacks	whites
Percent of births to unmarried women	65	20

G. Unemployment: 1992

	blacks	whites
16–19 years old (in thousands)	313	983
20–24 years old (in thousands)	401	1,084
16–19 years old (%)	39.8	17.1
20–24 years old (%)	23.9	9.4

H. Housing: 1990

	blacks	whites
Owner occupied	43.4	68.2

I. Law Enforcement, Courts and Prisons: 1991

	blacks	whites
Average number of inmates[3]	187,617	190,333
Prisoners executed under civil authority	7	7
Prisoners under sentence of death	1,018[4]	1,464

---

3. Excludes federal and state prisons, or other correctional institutions, institutions exclusively for juveniles, state operated jails in Alaska, Connecticut, Delaware, Hawaii, Rhode Island and Vermont; and other facilities which retain persons for less than 48 hours.

4. Including other people of color.

Index